T0283106

"Life is a package deal." These words were spoken by my dear friend, Ed Allen, in a speech delivered at his fortieth high school reunion. In this moving and compelling memoir, we learn that behind all the success, achievements, and accolades earned along the way as a very accomplished Naval Aviator, his is a story of a kind, courageous man who has endured loss and grief and personal and professional challenges to reach a place of grace and joy. Success and achievement are found not only on the medals displayed on one's chest but also in the hard work involved in overcoming life's struggles and challenges. In this memoir, we are privileged to share in the remarkable journey of a truly successful man.

—*Vice Admiral John Craine, USN (Ret.)*

I am delighted for all of us that Ed Allen has written his story. His wisdom, related in these pages and as a business advisor, helped to guide our company through rough waters to smooth sailing a decade ago. He mixes common sense, with lessons from extensive leadership experience and a deep sense of responsibility to help everyone he meets to be their best, and the results are a legacy of people who are very glad they know Ed. Stephanie and I have been blessed not only to know this man of faith but also to call him friend. I hope you will also get to know him as he tells his unlikely story that takes us from hard scrabble South Texas to the highest halls of power in our country. Only in America can *Oh Yeah? Watch This!* happen.

—*Bill Boisture, Former CEO, Hawker Beechcraft Corporation, and Partner, AE Industrial Partners*

Join me now as I briefly—all too briefly—paint the portrait of an oneirocritic man who has a reserved place in the pantheon for American heroes. Eddie Allen's genius in turning abstract theories into practical realities, his audacity in attempting what appears impossible and then succeeding, his perseverance in the face of adversities, his lofty family values, his indomitable faith and belief in God and country, his intense dedication, his infectious inspiration, and his demonstrated faith in blazing a path into the unknown are widely known and admired. Success is self-perpetuating—and you wrote the book on how to succeed and have many years of tremendous success behind you.

—*Vice Admiral Jerry O. Tuttle, USN (Ret.)*

(Note: Provided by his daughter, Vicky Tuttle, Admiral Tuttle has passed away. This excerpt is from his speech upon my Navy retirement.)

Knowing Ed Allen has been a life-changing experience for me. I've had the distinct privilege of working together with Ed on executive coaching and leadership development projects. Those projects were among the most gratifying of my career.

We saw teams transform, and we marveled at how rewarding it was to be a part of that experience. And the best part was getting to do that work with Ed. I could not have found a more competent, caring, completely authentic, humble, and absolutely hilarious compadre to work alongside. To this day, I continue to be inspired by Ed. I'm certain you will, too.

—*Jane Creswell, Executive Coach and Mentor*

This book chronicles the remarkable life journey of a gifted leader who generously shares his own story of adversity, failures, and successes—and in so doing provides a glimpse into what it means to be human. This is the story of one individual's drive to overcome the odds and be his best as he serves the nation, his family, and all those who had the benefit of his accumulated wisdom in his professional career. I am grateful to call Ed my friend and mentor.

—*Shawn Vick, Chairman, Global Jet Partners*

I have known Eddie Allen for over fifty-four years. We first met when I checked into my first U.S. Navy Fighter Squadron, VF 1. The squadron was blessed with a cadre of talented radar intercept officers (RIOs), some of the best I was ever privileged to fly with in my twenty years of Navy flying. Ed stood out in that group as an intelligent, savvy, and expert air warrior. I was not surprised to see Ed ascend to the highest leadership positions in the Navy. While Ed and I did not meet again until we were both captains in the late '80s, I followed his career with great interest. Ed had become the commanding officer of USS *Coral Sea*, and the ship had done exceedingly well in its operational evaluation. I was working on the staff of his boss who wanted to fly out to the ship as she returned to congratulate the crew. I went along and was able to see for myself how focused Ed was on completing the mission of his ship. After retirement from active duty, his intelligence, ability to understand the crux of a situation, devise, and execute the desired result ensured his continued success. At Oracle, he fell in love with coaching and became a truly great business coach, relying on his experiences and successes. Upon leaving Oracle, he started his own coaching company which has been sought after by many corporations, large and small. I have tremendous esteem for Ed and all he has accomplished. This book, while perhaps not a guidebook to success, describes how intelligence, drive, and focus will often yield great achievement.

—*Vice Admiral John Totushek, USN (Ret.)*

I have had the distinct privilege to have had Admiral Ed Allen in my life, first as a corporate coach, then as a mentor, and finally as a dear friend. Ed shared with me his experiences and wisdom, which have helped guide me through many challenging times in my life and quite frankly helped mold me into the person I am today. As reflected in this book, overcoming emotional hurdles, having a positive outlook on life, and living a life of commitment, duty, and honor while never taking yourself too seriously are the hallmarks of Ed Allen's journey.

—*Richard Emery, Dallas Business Executive*

The immediacy and joy of my first meeting with Admiral Ed Allen has never left me. His gravitas, his humor, his "blink,"

the enormous capacity to assess every detail in the moment—
it was clear why he won the Tailhook Award and had more
success in more Commands than anyone I knew. Our first
meeting took me back to "Friday Night Lights" in our shared
home state, and Ed was the one you wanted in the fourth
quarter when it looked really, really bad. He just had "It." He
was a warrior, an aviator, a loving family man, a Christian,
and the first choice for a comrade in arms and life (and the
fourth quarter down 6 points to Midland). There was no
"quit" in the man. His difficult, in many ways tragic, early
years honed his soul and created the capacity of excellence
and duty, and he gave it his all. He declined the opportunity
to be a victim of any adversity and grew clearer and stronger
than anyone I knew. The twinkle in his eye revealed the
humor, irony, and joy, which is perhaps the highest form of
wisdom. He never complained. He loved his God who gave
him the precious gift of life and lived with gratitude in his
heart for life and love and the opportunity to leave the camp-
ground a little better. He did. And he had more than a little
help from Saint Donna, his loving wife and peer!

—*Captain Ronald Earl Smith, MD PhD (Ret.) MC, USN*

Oh Yeah? Watch This! is a stunningly revealing self-description
of the life of a former boss, distinguished colleague, compas-
sionate mentor, and dearest friend of, now, more than forty-
five years. It is said that each of us is really two people, the
person we portray *outwardly*, sometimes with artifice and
bombast, and the person we really *are*, human beings shaped
by all the foibles, failings, hurts, and insecurities that coexist
even within a life ultimately marked by obstacles overcome,

career pinnacles reached, and love, both given and received, finally achieved. An old Irish proverb says, "It is in the shelter of each other that the people live." Countless associates, colleagues, and friends have taken shelter in Ed's deep wisdom, piercing insights, patient leadership, and unfailing encouragement, unaware that they welled from lifelong challenges and his deeply impactful and very personal experiences. He instinctively senses the feelings and emotions of others, we now see in hindsight, because he has walked an even more challenging and cyclic path through the valleys of both deep darkness and warming light. He has given selflessly of himself and, in so doing, enhanced the lives of thousands. This work only adds to that aura. Admiral Ed Allen has penned a courageous narrative that, while acknowledging the person that we all know, strips away the curtain to reveal the person starkly and emotionally I only caught glimpses of in our decades-long shared journey in the rough-and-tumble world of Navy fighter aviation and beyond. Ed has taken to heart Socrates' belief that the unexamined life is not worth living and reinforced the belief of the Stoic Epictetus that "[i]t is the difficulties that show what men are." But his style is not that of two dead Greeks. The story of his incredible journey is laid out in the unflinching manner of a fighter squadron post-flight debrief replete with the mandatory categories of "Good" and "Other" and is told with the wry humor that marks every successful fighter aviator. In the end, it is a story of both tragedy and triumph, told with both humility and quiet confidence, reminding all of us that, no matter how difficult the circumstances, we have the power within us to, simultaneously, both confront the sometimes-brutal reality of who or where we are and embrace the opportunity to shape a different future.

—*Admiral Jim Ellis, USN (Ret.)*

Eddie Allen is our hometown hero. He has earned a place among the most significant changemakers of our time. Beginning and ending in our hometown of Harlingen, Texas, his story grows from the depths of raw emotion surfacing from immeasurable tragedy and loss and takes us to heights of heart-stopping adventure in wild seas and dangerous skies. In between, we meet the man. All else becomes background. Eddie's is a tale of inner courage, emotional and physical survival, and, ultimately, peace, even in the midst of ever new challenges. This is the fascinating and important story of what makes Rear Admiral Ed Allen that hero, with lessons for us all. I couldn't put it down! Muchisimas gracias, mi amigo. Vaya con Dios!

—*Gerry MacPherson Fleuriet, President Harlingen High School Class of '61*

Ed Allen's journey from a childhood of trauma and adversity to Commanding Officer of one of our nation's attack carriers is both inspirational and instructive, demonstrating to all of us that perseverance and right thinking can and will prevail, a critical message in our present national moment where dysfunction threatens. All should hear and absorb Ed's message: stay the course, seek to achieve, and embody the right values. A story worth telling. More importantly, a story worth hearing. Thanks, high school buddy, for opening up and sharing.

—*Randy Fleuriet, a childhood and high school close friend*

It is with great pleasure that I write this testimonial for Ed Allen's memoirs, *Oh Yeah? Watch This!* I've had a close relationship with Ed, for eighteen years in uniform and the past twenty-three years in industry. So I am delighted to tell my story about how he has influenced me and others personally and professionally.

Ed came to Naval Air Station (NAS) Whidbey for an abbreviated syllabus as a Bombardier/Navigator in the A-6 Training Squadron, VA-128. After initial indoctrination in the A-6, Ed asked to fly some of his advanced Bombardier/ Navigator (B/N) training hops with me as his pilot. It was on those training flights that I recognized how Ed got his call sign "Bull Dog." He wasn't our routine prospective air wing Commander, most of whom were interested in learning basics of the A-6 Intruder and some B/N skills. Not Bull Dog. He was "all in" to employ the A-6 to the maximum of its capabilities. There were several low-level all-weather night missions where I'd be flying a bit slower and somewhat higher while flying at night in the deep valleys of the Cascade Mountains. Bull Dog would always call for faster and lower. I suggested he should get a few more hours in the A-6 before taking the Cascades on at high speed at 500 feet above the terrain. Bull Dog was having none of that. He was always quick to respond, "Hey Bud, trust me, I've got this!" I'd push the throttles up, move the stick forward, and say my prayers. I quickly learned Bull Dog was in his element, demonstrating strike warfare competence and courageous in-extremis leadership. For the next two years, we remained a tight A-6 crew, with CAG Allen as strike leader, innovating new tactics while leading major air wing missions from my right seat.

That bond continued over the next forty years throughout our Navy and private sector careers.

Why this book is important to all leaders and future leaders are the remarkable insights into Ed's leadership and how these traits translate to the success for elite business leaders operating in dangerous competitive environments. I am talking about the higher requirements of competence, trust, nonverbal communications, shared risk, expressions of genuine humility, and concern for others over self. These are essential character ingredients that inspire loyalty and courageous behaviors in others.

I am just one of dozens of Naval officers, sailors, and industry leaders who Ed inspired and maneuvered to far greater successes at work and in life. These most fortunate people are Ed Allen's greatest legacy.

—*Bud Langston, Senior Vice President, Salesforce*

I am honored to write this heartfelt testimonial for my friend and mentor, Ed Allen, and his extraordinary new book. Not only has Ed made a profound impact on my life through his mentorship, but his book has further deepened that influence, leaving an indelible mark on my journey of personal and intellectual growth. This book is evidence of his profound understanding of the human experience as he invites us on a transformative journey of self-discovery, compassion, and personal growth. I was mesmerized by the brilliance of his storytelling and his uncanny ability to captivate readers with his words. It is also a testament to his remarkable talent, unwavering dedication, and the extraordinary impact he has on the lives of those fortunate enough to know him.

—*Lisa DeMille, Global Vice President, Salesforce*

I have known Eddie since we were kids, and he is without a doubt one of the most accomplished persons I have ever known. He has always excelled in whatever he has done. You will enjoy reading about his life in this book. It is the story of a man who rose to the highest levels in the Navy and also in civilian life. While in the Navy, he was awarded the Tail-hooker of the Year Award as the aviator who did the most for naval aviation that year and also the John Paul Jones Award as the Commanding Officer of the most improved ship in the Navy. After his Navy retirement, he was a specialist as a coach for executives, advising them on how to further enhance their careers and business dealings.

—*John Fitzgerald, USNA Class of 1964*

While reading this masterful work, I realized that very little of Ed Allen's early life, let alone the "emotional baggage" that he was carrying beneath his radiant aura of confidence, was known to me. This was despite being "soulmates" for nearly a decade in a weekly 12-Step Program "knock off."

Ed is not an alcoholic/addict. But his powerful testament depicts the debilitating traits and habits as difficult as the challenges of those battling physical addictions. Among them is the debilitating tendency to engage obsessively in what the 12 Steps refer to as "stinking thinking," sometimes called the universal addiction.

Ed admitted that he was powerless and then began the process of letting go of the death grip on everything in his life. This is far easier said than done, especially for an accomplished Naval officer whose entire life was bound up in the belief that surrendering to one's limitations was tantamount to professional—and hence, personal—suicide.

Ed's work chronicles the life of a man willing to Let Go, Let God to follow a most difficult path toward emotional sobriety, which is our "saving grace."

—Colonel Larry Burgess, USMC (Ret.)

A great tale, well told. It is a story of an ordinary person interacting with ordinary people experiencing the gamut of human existence—tragedy, joy, depression, rejection, achievement, and failure. Ending in redemption and reflection on a life well lived. A must-read.

—Jeffrey W. Hurt Esq., USAFA class of 1967

I had the great fortune to serve with Ed Allen as his operations officer when he commanded the USS *Coral Sea*, then the oldest aircraft carrier in the Atlantic Fleet. I have served with both leaders and Commanders; Ed is the quintessential amalgam of both. He has the innate ability to build a strong and cohesive team, the intellect to articulate the mission clearly and precisely, and the experience and confidence to then allow you to do your job without superfluous "rudder orders." RADM Allen is the embodiment of the finest qualities that we seek in those who serve our country—and there is much one can learn from *Oh Yeah? Watch This!*

—*Captain Steve Counts, USN (Ret.)*

Eddie and I were football teammates at Harlingen High School. My dad was our coach. Dad often said his greatest satisfaction in coaching was not how his players performed on the field but what they accomplished after football. Football ends. Life goes on. Football teaches valuable lessons in overcoming adversity, reaching goals, teamwork, and leadership. I still remember Eddie's football picture in our yearbook. He had a look of dogged determination. Besides being highly intelligent and purpose-driven, Eddie is very likeable. He is always honest and reliable, has a hearty laugh, and is fun to be with. I am honored to call Eddie my friend. I had no idea about the hardships he was enduring before and through high school until I read his book—but that revelation highlighted another of his numerous qualities: Eddie never complained. Want to go on an amazing journey? Read Eddie's book!

—*Joe Hamrick Jr., high school football teammate*

Eddie Allen has been my friend and part of my family for over fifty-five years. We met in our first Fighter Squadron, VF-41, in 1967. We flew F-4s together, we experienced aircraft carrier operations for the first time, and we survived our first overseas deployment. *Oh Yeah? Watch This!* is a harbinger for the reader that anything is possible. No matter where you start on the totem pole of life, you can reach the top with hard work, going the extra mile, and determination. The author had a humble beginning in south Texas but rose to be a U.S. Navy Rear Admiral, a very successful businessman, and an executive coach. His life story is an example for all of us on the values of faith, courage, honesty, and commitment.

—*Captain John F. Manning Jr., USN (Ret.)*

After only four months of Ed's coaching, I was able to develop a highly focused statement of purpose for both my personal and business lives. Over the course of the next fifteen-plus years, this document became the cornerstone for major life decisions, including where to live and work. It also helped me prioritize my personal time to focus on my family, church, and community. Ed's coaching continues to have an instrumental influence on my many life and business successes. His coaching was so influential, I went back to college at fifty-five and became a coach too.

—*Dennis Francis, Coaching Client*

Eddie and I go back many decades, and since we met as Navy Ensigns, I've considered him an outstanding leader and a lifelong friend. As my RIO while I piloted an F-4 Phantom II, we depended on one another for our lives. Eddie captures a harrowing moment from our many adventures and shares so much more through from-the-heart storytelling of a well-lived life. If I fly an F-4 on one good engine and have Eddie in my back seat, I know I'm ok.

Eddie always exhibited outstanding leadership through his team spirit, astute decision-making, and being calm under pressure. I felt early on that Eddie would be "going places" and that he'd lead others to great places, too. Eddie was dedicated to being the best.

My wife, Brenda, and I were so impressed with how Eddie lived his life on a daily basis that we asked him to be the godparent of our eldest son. Eddie has great character, and anyone who reads this gem will find inspiration that perhaps the seemingly impossible is just a blip on the radar.

Jon A. McBride, Captain USN/NASA Space Shuttle Pilot (retired)

★ ★

OH YEAH? WATCH THIS!

OH YEAH? WATCH THIS!

★★

A RETIRED REAR ADMIRAL'S JOURNEY
FROM THE VALLEYS TO THE MOUNTAINTOPS

ED ALLEN

Advantage | Books

Published by Advantage Books, Charleston, South Carolina.
An imprint of Advantage Media.

ADVANTAGE is a registered trademark, and the Advantage colophon is a trademark of Advantage Media Group, Inc.

Printed in the United States of America.

10 9 8 7 6 5 4 3 2 1

ISBN: 978-1-64225-944-5 (Hardcover)
ISBN: 978-1-64225-943-8 (eBook)

Library of Congress Control Number: 2023916862

Cover and layout design by Matthew Morse.

Cover photo by Capt. C. J. Heatley III, USN (ret), Navy fighter pilot and TOPGUN Instructor. Authorized by CAPT Heatley.

Advantage Books is an imprint of Advantage Media Group. Advantage Media helps busy entrepreneurs, CEOs, and leaders write and publish a book to grow their business and become the authority in their field. Advantage authors comprise an exclusive community of industry professionals, idea-makers, and thought leaders. For more information go to **advantagemedia.com**.

I dedicate this book to Mimi, Jane, and Donna.
Mimi and Jane ensured that I had a Christian foundation.
Donna has shown me the meaning of love and home.

★ ★

CONTENTS

ACKNOWLEDGMENTS

To my many family members Allens, Hamners, Cooks, Lawsons, Watkins, and Bleys. You loved and strengthened the good in me and forgave the bad.

To my Navy ship mates and squadron mates, it was my honor to serve with all and to lead many.

To my business associates, especially at Hawker Beechcraft and my coaching clients, you allowed me to live my purpose and be at my best.

Several friends and associates provided invaluable support with advice, clarity, and encouragement. More importantly, you patiently helped with editing, revising, and rephrasing which made the difference between good writing and great writing: my wife, Donna, my daughter-in-law Bobbi Cook, Randy Fleuriet, Gerry Fleuriet, John Craine, Johnny Fitzgerald, Patsy German Byfield. The following helped me recall and better describe Navy carrier flight operations: Bud Langston, Mike McCabe, Winston Copeland, Dave Crocker.

To God's greatest gift, my wife and best friend, Donna. You taught me about real love (1 Corinthians 10:13) and family. I honor and pay tribute to you with these Old Hymns: "How Great Thou Art,"

"Because He Lives," "Bless the Lord O My Soul," "What A Friend We Have In Jesus," and "Jesus Loves Me."

To the Trinity of the Christian faith, the Father, the Son, and the Holy Spirit. During this writing, I have experienced a greater and stronger understanding and meaning of the Cross, grace, and unending love.

FOREWORD

I was deeply honored when I was asked to write the foreword for *Oh Yeah? Watch This!* First, because the author is a good friend and a peer whom I respect and admire for his honesty, integrity, and devotion to duty as a U.S. Navy officer. Second, because he embodies the finest qualities of the American national character upon which this nation was built, qualities that sometimes seem to be sorely lacking in many leaders today.

Ed Allen came from humble beginnings in a border town in the Rio Grande Valley of south Texas and, through strong will, tenacity, and determination, ascended to the highest ranks of leadership in the Navy. It is no surprise to those in the naval aviation fighter community who know him well why his "call sign" became "Bull Dog." Attesting to his qualities of leadership, in 1990 Ed was selected as the recipient of two prestigious awards—the U.S. Navy League's John Paul Jones Award and the Tailhook Association's Tailhooker of the Year Award.

Ed's story is one of inspiration, achievement, heartache, and emotion. *Oh, Yeah? Watch This!* chronicles that journey with a cathartic, no-holds-barred narrative of all the ups, downs, thrills, and disappointments that only one who took that journey could know. Ed writes of the anxieties of his early childhood and the triumphs, as well as the missteps, that marked his rise from ensign to Rear Admiral. One's life and career aren't always what it might seem when looking at it from the outside. This book tells a story full of courage, truth, commitment, and closure.

I've been privileged to know Ed for over forty years, and I'm proud to call him a good friend and "shipmate." While we only had one opportunity to actually serve together at the Pentagon later in our careers, our paths crossed many times during the course of our Navy careers. Ed and I are both Naval Flight Officers (NFO) and flew as a radar intercept officer (RIO) in the F-4 Phantom and the F-14 Tomcat fighters. We sometimes paralleled and sometimes followed each other in our flying careers. For instance, Ed received orders out of Fighter Squadron One (VF-1) in June 1976, and I joined VF-1 in November 1976. Then in the early 1980s, when I was Commanding Officer of fighter squadron VF-114, Ed was Commanding Officer of VF-1. Following our squadron command tours, we both received orders to attend the National Defense University—Ed being enrolled in the National War College and me in the Industrial College of the Armed Forces. Both schools being on the same campus at Ft. McNair in Washington, District of Columbia, we saw each other frequently. That time, both of us were avid runners, and we trained together to run the U.S. Marine Corps (USMC) Marathon in the District of Columbia.

I first met Ed in the Navy aviation fighter community in 1974 at the Naval Air Station (NAS) Miramar in San Diego, California. Ed had been selected to join a highly respected cadre of Naval Aviators charged with standing up the first two squadrons of the Navy's newest fighter, the F-14 Tomcat, and integrating it into the fleet. The year prior, in March 1973, I had just returned from being a prisoner of war (POW) in Vietnam, and when we met, I was executive officer

(XO) of the Navy Fighter Weapons School (Top Gun) at Miramar. Ed was actively involved in developing tactics to take advantage of the F-14's formidable capabilities as a fighter aircraft. Those tactics would eventually be incorporated into the Top Gun syllabus to instruct F-14 aircrews when they started attending the school.

During our time in the Navy, I had no idea of what emotional baggage Ed might have been carrying. As it turns out, he became a master at being able to compartmentalize emotions and never let his personal life problems interfere with his carrying out the responsibilities of his professional life. Ed was a great leader, always outwardly upbeat, affable, and straightforward in his dealings with his Navy peers and subordinates—belying whatever may have been going on under the surface. It wasn't until I read *Oh, Yeah? Watch This!* that I came to know the emotional roller coaster my good friend Ed had been riding and had managed to control for so many years as he rose through the ranks in the demanding and dangerous profession of naval aviation.

In this book, you see a man daily facing increasingly demanding jobs with courage, commitment, humor, and intelligence, all the while keeping his deep, disturbing emotions submerged. The charm of this book is the fact that originally it was probably not written to be read by others. But this introspective into the heart and soul of a man is deeply moving, and it can serve as a guide for others who may be facing similar circumstances in life.

—*Capt. Jack Ensch, USN (Ret.)*

A VIEW FROM HIGHER GROUND

Life is about our stories, and this is mine.

It is a story about:

- an infant, born amid tragedy and chaos, but whose aunt loved and nurtured him;
- a boy playing hide and seek, hugging a puppy, singing old hymns, joining Boy Scouts;
- a young man playing football, falling in love, and the dignity of hard work;
- a Navy ensign flying in jets from aircraft carriers and achieving the rank of Rear Admiral;
- a man who found the meaning of love and success beyond his dreams;
- a flawed man committed to living a Christ-centered life.

It is also a story about:

- a toddler who experienced an "authorized" kidnapping;
- a scared, abused lonely boy, ridiculed by his broken father;
- a confused and defiant teenager desperate for acceptance;
- a young man lacking self-confidence in search of an identity;
- a man whose father was lost in emotional pain and whose son's achievements were the primary source of his pride;
- a man who demonstrated some poor judgment, which affected personal and professional success.

I have experienced valleys and mountaintops. The valleys were deep and long, and the struggles were many. On my climb to higher ground, I often slipped and fell but always got up and grew stronger to where, at long last, I could see the view. And what lay before me wasn't the world of troubles that I'd known. It was the beauty of rolling hills.

I understand now that to appreciate the mountaintops, I needed to experience the valleys. For years, I met the challenges of naysayers with the defiance and hubris of *"Oh Yeah? Watch This!"* I was in charge, with high energy and fierce resolve and determined to achieve and succeed. I was the Captain of my mighty warship and totally in command. Along the way, I've learned to listen more than talk—and discovered that the ultimate success comes with patience and forgiveness, living by faith, trust, and to better know who is the real Captain. It's not me.

SOUTH OF KINGSVILLE

On September 30, 2001, just after the horrific 9/11 attacks, my wife, Donna, and I were driving from Dallas to my hometown of Harlingen, Texas, deep in the Rio Grande Valley of south Texas. My visits back to Harlingen had been infrequent, mostly for a wedding or funeral. On this occasion, I had been asked to speak at my fortieth high school class reunion.

I dreaded each trip, particularly the last ninety miles of Highway 77 south of Kingsville. I felt as barren as the landscape of mesquite trees and brush as we crossed the empty expanse of the King Ranch between Kingsville and Harlingen, Texas. Every monotonous mile was bringing me closer to my past.

At the Harlingen city limits, I took the "Sunshine Strip" bypass through some old neighborhoods, past landmarks that I had seen only a few times since leaving nearly four decades earlier. As I drove, I recalled special times and cherished friendships. I thought of football and camping, of hunting with my buddies, of hours spent on the beaches. And then the other memories came back, and my reverie faded.

Along the way, we passed Tri-Pak Machinery Service, a manufacturer of vegetable packing machinery where my dad had been vice president and general manager for forty-three years. There, at age ten, covered in grease and sweat in the hot Texas sun, I disassembled old machinery for salvage, earning fifteen cents an hour. Mr. J. R. Fitzgerald, owner of Tri-Pak, gave me a raise to thirty cents per hour the following year. His son, Johnny, and I are close friends to this day.

I had been reluctant to accept the invitation to speak at the reunion. Donna encouraged me to reconsider despite my anxiety. "You must do this, Eddie," she said. "You've had a rich life, and you have a responsibility to share it with so many classmates who love and respect you. You have no right not to go."

As a former Navy Rear Admiral, I had not worn my uniform, the "cloth of the nation," for several years, but my classmates, nonetheless, felt this was a particularly compelling time to hear my story. In the milieu after the 9/11 attacks, the public thought of firefighters, police, and first responders as heroes. The class of 1961 wanted to hear from their own Eddie Allen, who had flown in F-4's and F-14 fighters and led six commands including an aircraft carrier and a Carrier Battle Group.

Yes, I had amounted to something, after all. I found a home in the Navy and a good deal of success there. After retiring, I began a second career at the Oracle Corporation, where I was a vice president for defense business development. Already in my late fifties at the turn of the millennium, I was beginning to see how these military and corporate experiences, both the successes and failures, had been preparing me for something else. I was closer to discovering and living my life purpose.

Looking off to my right, I smiled upon seeing the football field at Harlingen High School. I recalled those long summer "two-a-days" of practice in the humid Texas heat, followed by a root beer float at the local

A&W. Football was for me the game of life and still it is. I developed strength and confidence and learned the value of teamwork. The names of those teammates came streaming back to me: Jimmy Jondahl and Henry Roberts; Lonnie Davis and Jimmy Dale; Joe Hamrick, Butch Palmer, Don Madden—I could still see their faces and hear their shouts as we charged across the field. Jimmy and I were close friends. I joined the Navy; he joined the Air Force. He was killed during flight training in a T-38 Talon accident. He was my close friend, and then he was gone.

East of town, we passed Valley International Airport, which was once an Air Force base and now a commercial airport and home to the Marine Military Academy. I thought back to my earliest memory of flight. I have a crinkled photograph of a towheaded five-year-old boy in coveralls, climbing into a Stearman biplane. That was me. My dad was a pilot who flew both for his business and for pleasure, and that was my first flight. There would be many more.

Shortly after my sixteenth birthday, I soloed at the Harlingen airport. In flight, I felt comfortable. I felt at home. I rode my bicycle every Saturday morning to the airport, spending hours washing and waxing the airplanes in return for the opportunity to join the pilots on short local flights. I can still recall the unique smell of the cockpits— fuel, oil, and polish. The highlight was a flight in a navy-blue Beechcraft Bonanza, with a V-tail, a throw-over yoke, and retractable landing gear. I remember that flight more than any other.

Approaching the Arroyo Colorado bridge on the bypass, Donna and I were getting closer to our hotel. I took note of East Taylor Street as we passed it. I looked down the row of houses toward the one where I had lived as a teenager. Most memories associated with that house were painful. A little farther south, I glanced down the street to see the home of one of my high school girlfriends. Our time together was filled with smiles, laughs, and dreams. Finally, with much sadness, I

11

had realized that a life together was not meant to be, and I went off to college. Driving farther south, I noticed the Golden Palms nursing home where my dad spent his final days.

In the distance, I could see grain and cotton fields. In the summers, I drove a big John Deere grain combine at a family farm for a dollar an hour, wearing bandanas around my face and neck to protect against the chaff. At lunchtime, sitting with the Mexican laborers, I often would trade my bologna sandwich for a tamale. We each thought we were getting the better deal.

"What are you planning to do when you get out of high school?" one of the men on the crew asked me during a break.

"I don't know," I answered, "but it's not going to be this." I didn't mind the work, but I had a sense of purpose for something different. I knew two things: I had a special life to live, and it probably would not be south of Kingsville.

The reunion dinner was scheduled for the evening after we arrived. Donna and I proceeded to the country club, where I reminisced with my classmates on our times of joy and pain. There were many warm hugs with the ladies and hearty backslapping with the men, especially my former teammates.

After dinner, a dear friend and classmate, Randy Fleuriet, introduced me as speaker. He eloquently hit the highlights of my Navy career: several fighter squadron tours; Commander of an Air Wing and Captain of the amphibious assault ship USS *Vancouver* (LPD-2); Captain of the aircraft carrier USS *Coral Sea* (CV-43); promotion to Rear Admiral; and command of the Naval Space Command, a Carrier Battle Group, and the North Atlantic Treaty Organization (NATO) Strike Force. My shore duty included four tours in the Pentagon, including Deputy Director for Current Operations for the Joint Chiefs of Staff, led by Gen. Colin Powell.

I felt honored yet humbled by his introduction, with more acclaim than I felt I deserved. Now all eyes were on me as I stood at the podium. The silence was palpable. I had organized my speech around the words of Solomon from Ecclesiastes—"for everything there is a season, and a time for every purpose under heaven." That ancient wisdom embodies the themes of life that I have long observed and that have come up time and time again in my relationships with family, friends, shipmates, and business associates.

Recently I found my old copy of that speech. Here is an excerpt:

> *During these forty years, each of us experienced a different journey. However, we experienced many of the same passages in life—the joys of love, marriage, family, children, grandchildren. holidays, birthdays, anniversaries, weddings, and funerals. We assumed many roles as family members, parents, homemakers, teachers, businessmen and women. We served in government, health, and educational institutions. We experienced life and happiness in many ways.*
>
> *But life is a package deal. Along with love, joy, grace, success and achievement, there are setbacks and disappointments. We experienced pain, suffering and loss—the loss of family and friends, professional failures, accidents, addictions, divorce, cancer, and death.*
>
> *And now, through all this, we come together to tell our stories and to recall our times together.*

Life is indeed a package deal, and each of us has a story to tell about how we have experienced the seasons. My classmates had known me at age seventeen. Who was I now? What had really become, and what was becoming, of Eddie Allen?

CHAPTER 1

A TIME TO BE BORN AND A TIME TO DIE

I have a fading photograph of a young man and a woman on the beach at South Padre Island, Texas. He has lifted her high into his arms. "Put me down!" her expression shouts, and his face shines with delight. This is the intimacy and joy of newlyweds. It is a tableau of what was and of what might have been.

The couple was my father and mother, Lloyd and Mahalah Allen, enjoying their moment in the sun not long after their wedding day. The world was at war. In just a few months, he would leave to serve in the Army infantry.

In my mind's eye is another scene, a vivid one that will not fade. A young soldier gazed out the window at the shifting scenery. That soldier was my dad, a twenty-five-year-old Second Lieutenant. He was headed to Houston on a few days' leave from Fort Stewart, Georgia, after getting a telegram that his wife was in labor. The trip was nearly nine hundred miles, mostly on two-lane roads, and the wartime speed limit was thirty-five miles an hour. Unable to sleep in the cramped bus seat, he leaned on his duffel bag. His thoughts were racing. In a few weeks, he would be shipping out to the Western Pacific. He was excited about seeing his wife and new baby—but would he ever see them again? On a brief layover in New Orleans, he got out to stretch and get a bite to eat. Two nuns from a local church approach and whisper something to him. "Are you Lt. Lloyd Allen?" one of them asked. "Yes," my dad said. He squinted in the sunshine. "How do you know me?" The other nun gave him the news: "Lt. Allen, we've been asked to meet you here and deliver a message. Your wife delivered a healthy baby boy at St. Joseph's Hospital in Houston. The baby is fine, but ... your wife didn't make it." The young soldier's face registers confusion, then disbelief, and then horror. It is November 19, 1943, the day that I was born.

It was one of those shattering moments when the world stops. Life would never be the same. Soon he would climb back on the bus, shocked, dazed, and alone with strangers, with miles to go and no hope of sleep. And soon a nurse would be placing a squalling infant in his arms. The love of his life was gone, and here was a new life for which he was responsible.

As for me, I was blissfully ignorant of anything but hunger, and that is why I cannot explain, to this day, why I have within me something that resembles a memory, with details beyond what an infant could possibly observe. You might call it a dream. To me, it is true and real. I am lying in my bassinet at the hospital. I am aware, somehow, that a man and a woman are standing a few feet away. I do not know who they are. They are dressed in the style of the 1940s. She wears a victory suit and a pillbox hat, and he holds a fedora over his double-breasted jacket. As they gaze into my crib, the woman whispers softly to the man, "Isn't that too bad?" Together, they shake their heads solemnly side to side.

That is a message imprinted on my heart and soul. Something was *too bad*, and it must be me. I felt that the world would have been a better place had I never shown up. My birth did not engender joy. I represented loss, death, and mourning.

A Fitting Farewell

Fast forward to 1999, the year my father died, and to the country cemetery in south Texas where he lies buried. I wish to honor him in this book, for he was part of the "Greatest Generation," but that honor must come with an honest assessment of the role he played in my life.

A father has the power to motivate his son or wound him. Mine did both. I know he loved me, as best he knew how. He was also a demanding, angry, abusive man. My compulsion to succeed arose partly from a desire to disprove his harsh disapprovals. If he was proud of my accomplishments, it was more about him than me.

I was able to forgive my dad after he passed, but this was possible only after much prayer. I had to let go of judging and blaming him and first confess that I, too, had shown disrespect and defiance. I forgave him, and I asked to be forgiven.

At his funeral, I spoke of his love of country, family, and friends, and of his appreciation for the military, having served as an Army Captain during World War II in the Pacific. I told of his forty-three-year career with Tri-Pak and of his love for flying. These are excerpts from my eulogy for Lloyd Allen, my dad:

> *He had a childlike curiosity and intensity about life that revealed his wonder and appreciation for God's creation. He loved the outdoors,*

especially hunting and fishing. He tied his own fishing flies and loaded his own ammo. He always had a hobby, which at various times included raising cattle, photography, growing flowers, making jewelry, painting Texas landscapes and dogs, working with ceramics, and writing fiction. He loved to read and valued his hundreds of books as much as his guns, which says a lot about this man with a Texas Ranger heritage.

He was clearly the "head of the household," and his top priority was to provide a home with emphasis on education for his children. These goals were not a "given" for that Depression generation. He did not attend college, but all three of his children did, and earned bachelor's and/or master's degrees.

He taught me three things about business: work hard (the extra mile is not very crowded), give your customers good value, and take care of the "men and women in the shop." Those three values were part of the foundation of my Navy leadership, especially as Captain of the USS Coral Sea (CV-43).

At his graveside that day, the Veterans of Foreign Wars formed an honor guard, read a proclamation honoring his military service, fired a twenty-one-gun salute, and played taps. Then I handed out brightly colored helium balloons to each of the more than two hundred people attending the funeral. After a short last tribute, we released them and watched as they glided away, flying low and fast over the Texas countryside. I let go of a balloon that day—and much more.

Late that afternoon, six of us went for a flight in Tri-Pak's Cessna 421. We toured South Padre Island and then did a flyby at the cemetery around sunset for a final farewell to my father as he "headed west."

★ ★

CHAPTER 2

"SHE WAS A WONDERFUL PERSON..."

"There is a time for every purpose under heaven," Solomon wrote. On the day of my birth, a life began, and a life ended. The miracle of a first breath was mingled with the sorrow of a young woman passing into eternity. Something else slipped away that day—the dream of a family. The one that my dad had desired and that I was denied.

Consumed in grief, my dad faced several life-and-death decisions in just a few days. The love of his life was gone. He had to make the funeral and burial arrangements. What name would go on the birth certificate for his new baby son? He knew that in a few weeks, he would be deploying to the Western Pacific but didn't know when or even if he was coming back. Who would give little Eddie a home? Whose face would represent love and security?

My dad made the best decision possible. He left me in the care of my mother's brother, my Uncle Joe Ed Hamner ("Papa Joe") and his wife, Rosamond, known as "Mimi." They had a four-year-old daughter,

Peggy, and later would have a son, Dick, younger than I. They lived in Hempstead, about fifty miles northwest of Houston. Mimi, Papa Joe, and little Peggy loved me as their own. Mimi was a kind and nurturing mother figure, and Papa Joe was a source of strength and confidence. Hempstead was my home, and in the innocence of those few brief years, I felt safe and secure. Until I did not.

After arranging for my care, my dad returned to Fort Stewart and learned that his deployment had been deferred. During that brief time, he met Jane Hack in Hinesville, Georgia. Before leaving for the Pacific, he proposed to her.

When he returned, they got married and moved to East Buchanan Street in Harlingen. Before my birth, he and my mother had bought a small house there where they lived until he joined the Army and she moved to Houston to be with family during her pregnancy. Now, almost three years later, my father determined that it was time to move back to that house and commence the happy family life he had envisioned. It was now time for Eddie to come "home."

An Authorized Kidnapping

One Sunday afternoon, three strangers showed up in Hempstead. They were my paternal grandmother, her sister, and my fifteen-year-old cousin Gene. They had come to take me to Harlingen to live with my dad and my new "mommy." I was told that I was "going for a ride." It was a ride, all right—a one-way ride of 350 miles to Harlingen.

That was it. No explanations, no time to get acquainted. I would later refer to what happened as an "authorized kidnapping." Though I was only almost three years old, I somehow seem to recall that day. Whether it's a true memory or a flight of fancy, I can't say. But the image is vivid, and I have often returned to that moment, an observer of my own past. I see a '42 Chevy pulling away from a familiar house. A little boy pounds on the rear window, silently screaming as the car disappears.

So began a long journey filled with fear, confusion, and insecurity. Mimi, Papa Joe, and Peggy had been my world, a bright innocent one filled with love. Now that world had gone dark. I would not see them again for six years.

My new "mother," Jane Hack, was a kind, gentle, well-read, young Christian woman. She had a good heart but lacked the social skills to deal with the cultural shock associated with moving from Georgia to south Texas. She was starting a marriage without friends or family nearby and suddenly became responsible for raising a three-year-old. You might say she went from the Rhett Butler world of Georgia to the "J.R." world of Texas. Regardless of this overwhelming change, she did her best to be a wife, a mother, and a homemaker for my father and me. She always stood up for me but was no match for my father. I felt nothing but affection and gratitude toward her, and for her life I am grateful.

Jane's mother Ethel was, by contrast, a mean-hearted woman who became yet another new "grandmother" in my world. She was the matriarch of the Hack family whose southern aristocratic roots ran deep. Displayed prominently in the family living room was a framed coat of arms for the Daughters of the American Revolution. And now her well-bred daughter had married a commoner from Texas.

The Hack family's main business was timbering. In the early 1950s, the family expanded its business to include part of an island off the coast of South Carolina—an island called Hilton Head. I spent part of several summers there with my cousins and still cherish memories of those times, despite the overriding presence of grand-mother Ethel. Her resentment of me was palpable. "Remember your place!" she told me more than once. She made it clear that I would never be adopted, included in the will, or would share in any inheritance. I didn't understand and frankly didn't care. Still don't.

A Visit by Two Strangers

When I was about nine, Mimi and Papa Joe came back into my life. They drove to Harlingen to see my dad and to meet Jane. I was at Boy Scout Camp Perry near Harlingen at the time, so the four of them came unannounced to visit me briefly.

I still had not been told about the circumstances of my birth and of my mother's death. Jane Hack was the only mother I knew, and I was OK with that. Mimi and Papa Joe, who had treated me as their own, were strangers to me by then.

I still recall that meeting at the camp. I felt a warm connection with Mimi. When she hugged me, I felt safe and protected. I didn't want to leave her side. Something felt right, and I had no idea why. Years later, Mimi told me, "It tore my heart out because you looked so confused."

And I *was* confused. I was associated with three family names—the Allens, the Hamners, and the Hacks—but didn't understand the relationships. Mimi and Papa Joe would come to visit for a few hours and then disappear. I had no explanation. I imagined that I was in a zoo where people could come and stare at me and snap a picture. I imagined Mimi and Papa Joe returning home, wherever that was, and showing pictures of their zoo trip—and one of those pictures was of me. *See this one? It looks just like a shy little boy!*

I don't know how the agreement was reached, but soon thereafter, I would spend two or three weeks each summer in Hempstead with the Hamners. I would get to see Mimi, Papa Joe, cousin Peggy, and new younger cousin Dick, but I was also expected to spend a few days with my Hamner grandparents, who were the parents of my birth mother, Mahalah.

My dad would have preferred that I stay with the grandparents during those summer trips and that the other family members could visit me there. They only lived five miles apart, but the emotional distance was as far as east is from west. Tensions still lingered within the Hamner family over my dad's decision to leave me with Mimi and Papa Joe at my birth. Though it was the best decision he ever made on my behalf, it was a divisive one.

"Her Name Was Mahalah ..."

By then, I was starting to ask questions. I was trying to piece together the family relationships but couldn't solve the puzzle. Something wasn't right. I had an assortment of grandparents, aunts, uncles, and cousins, but I couldn't figure out the connections between the Hamners, Allens, and Hacks.

It was time for me to know the truth. Though it was my dad's responsibility to explain this to me, he somehow lacked the courage or composure to discuss it. Instead, he asked Mimi to tell me about the circumstances of my birth and who my mother was.

During my next visit to Hempstead, Mimi took me into the family room, opened a cabinet, and took out a silver frame with the picture of a beautiful woman. I studied her face. I sensed a connection with her.

"Eddie, this is your real mother," Mimi said. "Her name was Mahalah, and she died when you were born."

I looked into the eyes of the woman in the silver frame, struggling to comprehend those words. I glanced up at Mimi and then back at the photograph, and I began to sob. Mimi put her arms around me and just held me, and I cried until there was nothing left. My world had shattered. I was confused, scared, and devastated.

All I had wanted was to be safe and part of a "normal" family. I knew now that I was not part of the Hack family. I was a Hamner but without a Hamner mother. How did I fit in? "Am I part of the Hamner family?" I asked Mimi, months later. "Well, honey child," she answered, smiling a bit mischievously, "You're hanging on the family tree." That was sufficient then—and still is.

Several weeks after Mimi told me the truth, I sat in silence next to my father as we drove east through the Rio Grande Valley between La Feria and Harlingen in his green and white '53 Chevrolet. We were returning home from a call to one of his machinery customers in Weslaco. I gazed sullenly out the window as the late afternoon sun cast shadows across our path in the valley.

"Did Rosamond tell you about your mother?" he asked, breaking the silence.

"Yes sir, she did." I knew I had to answer, but I kept it at that. I adjusted my sun visor and focused on the horizon. Then I glanced over at him. He was staring straight ahead with his hands firmly gripping the steering wheel at ten and two. And then he said five words, the only words he ever expressed to me about my mother Mahalah:

"She was a wonderful person."

That was it. The silence resumed, and I didn't ask him to tell me more. Never again did he say anything to me about her or about my birth. Never did I ask. We were two souls bonded by a tragedy too painful to recount.

A Nurturing Spirit

Still, I wanted to know more about my mother. What made her wonderful? What made her laugh, and what made her cry? What brought joy, and what brought pain? Over several years, I filled in some details. Most of this came from Mimi, but I heard some of it from other family members and my mother's close friends.

I learned this about Mahala Hamner Allen: She had a deep faith and was active in the Methodist Church. She was a professional woman, a manager at the Central Power and Light Company in Harlingen. She was kind but firm and had no place for disrespect or pettiness. She had clear expectations and boundaries for my dad. A careful shopper, she had only a few dresses, but they were top quality. She had a quick wit and wicked sense of humor, which I inherited— sort of a self-deprecating take on *The Far Side*. She loved little children and puppy dogs.

I often wonder what my life would have been like if she had lived. I can guess. She would have protected me from my dad. I might have had more patience and less anger and developed emotional intelligence much sooner. She would have given me more of what I needed: more tough love, discipline, protection, a sharper sense of right and wrong. Comforted by her recognition and affirmations at home, perhaps I wouldn't have felt such a compulsion to achieve in life, to prove myself worthy. But that is all conjecture. I cannot know these things for. In his poem "Desiderata," Max Ehrmann wrote, "[T] he universe is unfolding as it should." I believe that.

Through the years, I have sensed her presence. The most dramatic incident was in 1998 while I was seated in a plane as it taxied for takeoff at Washington Dulles Airport. It was a cool morning with blue skies. I was headed to Boston on a business trip. I had just retired from the Navy and was a business development executive at the Oracle Corporation. I was in seat 12A, just forward of the left wing—that's how vividly I recall the scene.

I had been working at the time with a counselor, seeking clarity on a couple of unresolved life issues. The counselor was a wise, seasoned professional. She challenged me to write a letter to my mother, Mahalah, and tell her about my life and how I felt. And now, as the plane headed down the runway, I felt an almost involuntary motivation to write. I opened my portfolio, and the words flowed from my pen. Soon, I felt her response. I told her that I missed her. I told her about my loneliness. I told her that much of the time I had felt that I didn't belong, that I'd been abandoned. And I filled her in on my many accomplishments and honors and hoped she would be proud of me. The thoughts were coming *through* me but not *from* me. Her words were gentle, kind, loving, and encouraging. They were also firm with clear expectations. She regretted not having the opportunity to be with me—to love, protect, discipline, and challenge. *You were conceived and born with anticipation, joy, and gratitude, and I love you for eternity. But I was also concerned about your coming into a world at war.*

The letter was clear enough. She did not expect me to achieve great accomplishments or collect impressive honors. I didn't need to be the biggest, the best, the fastest, or the greatest. I just needed to be true to myself and live my purpose.

She closed with some loving but firm words: *Listen to me, Eddie. Don't you dare use my death to feel sorry for yourself, or feel entitled, or let the chaos and fear that you experienced as a child be an excuse for not being the man you should be. Remember that you are my legacy.*

In gratitude, I strive to meet her expectations. For too long, I tried to justify my birth, believing that it was my responsibility to live so that others would see me as significant. After all, a heavy price had been paid for my coming into this world.

My mother was telling me to be all I should be, to do all that I should do—and now I understood that she didn't mean attaining worldly honors and status. I should be defined by other measures. I deserved to live, and I didn't have to prove it to anyone and certainly not to her. I saw what I must cast away and what was mine to keep. I finally told that whispering couple who had peered so long into my hospital bassinet that they must go away—and they did.

CHAPTER 3

THE EMOTIONAL RANGE WAR

I awoke to the familiar sounds of shouting in the next room. "Either she goes, or I go!" I heard my dad yell, followed by slapping and muffled sobs. I clutched my covers and stared into the darkness. I was about fourteen years old, and this wasn't the first time I had heard my dad fighting with Jane, whose mother had come to visit. But it would be the last time.

"Get in the car, boy, now," Dad ordered a moment later as he appeared at my bedroom door. *Had I heard those words somewhere before?* I obeyed. I have no idea where we went or any memory at all of the next few days. I recall only the utter darkness of that night.

Soon afterward, Jane took Janet and Meg, my sisters, for the annual summer visit to Hinesville, Georgia. I wasn't invited this time. While they were away, my dad filed for divorce and notified Jane that she and the girls were not to return to Harlingen. Jane and her brother came back only to pack up.

"In Georgia, we just don't treat our women this way," the brother saw fit to mutter at me as he loaded a truck with the memories of a marriage. I felt only numbness, punctuated with guilt, fear, and confusion. I didn't belong. I had never belonged.

Summers in Hempstead

I lived in anticipation of annual summer visits to Hempstead. For those few summer weeks, I was with family, as family should be. I felt secure and accepted. It was more than just a reprieve from Harlingen. At my aunt and uncle's home, I felt safe being a kid.

I played baseball and football with my buddies. We rode bikes and swam, played with our dogs, went to matinees, and swung high in tire swings under the oaks. And at day's end, a home awaited me, a real one, with the happiness and acceptance that every child should know. I felt like a son to Mimi and Papa Joe and like a brother to Peggy and Dick. This was not a perfect family, but it was an authentic one.

Nor was this the perfect society as the decade of the 1950s sometimes is portrayed. To me, all seemed well on those Saturday afternoons when I would walk with a young friend to the movie theater to see westerns with Roy Rogers, the Lone Ranger, John Wayne, or Gary Cooper. A dime would get us admission, with a penny left over to buy a piece of candy. But the theater, like so many other establishments, had separate water fountains and rest rooms marked "white" and "colored." And I couldn't sit next to my friend. His skin color relegated him to the balcony, to which he retreated without question, at least outwardly. It all seemed so normal at the time. I didn't know what I didn't know. I'd like to think our culture has come a long way since those days. I know we still have a good way to go.

Particularly on Sundays during those summer visits, I looked forward to our routine of church, food, and fun. We attended the Methodist Church where Mimi played the piano and organ and sang from the hymnal the songs that became forever dear to me: "Great Is Thy Faithfulness," "How Great Thou Art," "The Old Rugged Cross," and my favorite, "Amazing Grace." After church, it was home for Sunday dinner at noon. Mimi had gotten up early to prepare it before we left for church. The meal was the same almost every Sunday, and to this day is my favorite—pot roast, mashed potatoes and gravy, homemade biscuits, green beans, and ambrosia and cherry pie for dessert. After dinner, I played with the neighborhood kids. No fear, no guilt, just fun.

Three or four days during the visit were spent with my Hamner grandparents, who lived on a small ranch about five miles north of Hempstead. Their home lacked plumbing, running water, and electricity. A typical day's routine included getting up at 5:30 for breakfast in the dining room. Grandma had risen about four o'clock in the morning to prepare a hearty breakfast of eggs, ham, or bacon and biscuits and gravy on a wood stove.

As Grandpa and I finished eating, Grandma would head to the barn to saddle our horses and lead them to the house. She was waiting there with them when we walked out on the porch. When I was little, I would ride with Grandpa, holding tight to the saddle horn. Later I had my own horse, a beautiful animal, and though he was no Secretariat, he was mine. We would head out on horseback to take care of the livestock, mend fences, and do other farm chores. Grandma had lunch waiting for us when we returned. As we ate, she took the horses to the corral to water, feed, and brush.

We took an afternoon nap, did a few chores, and then, late in the afternoon, sat in rocking chairs on the gallery for the evening's "event." A railroad ran parallel to the farm, and we could see far down the tracks. We knew that if the train was on schedule, it would pass by at 5:58 p.m. We would sit there ten minutes ahead of time, watch the flags go up, and know the train was coming. The warning flags went down after the train passed. When that part of the evening's entertainment was over, we would light a kerosene lantern and play cards or checkers.

I was happy visiting with my grandparents in the country and have many fond memories of being there, but where I belonged was in town with Mimi and Papa Joe. After another few days of playing and enjoying life, it was back to Harlingen. Mimi said that about forty-eight hours before I had to leave, I would become quiet and withdrawn, refusing to say much. It was back to living with uncertainty and fear.

One of my favorite sayings is, "You only need one." Yes, a stable family with a mother and father is the ideal, and I believe that is what God intended. But for me, Mimi was "the one" who loved me, believed in me, encouraged me—and whose example taught me to encourage others. My aunt was always there with a hug or a spankin' or whatever I needed on any given day. I can still see "the look" when I misbehaved. I knew what that meant. In the embrace of her love and reassurance, I began to feel safe and self-confident. She was my anchor then and for all my days to come.

The Casualties of War

During the twelve years that my dad and Jane were married, they had two children, Janet and Meg, six and nine years younger than I, respectively. Janet and Meg were considered part of the Hack family. I was not part of that circle. Nonetheless, Janet, Meg, and I got along well as siblings. They loved me as their big brother. The emotional barrier between us didn't arise from within. It was imposed from the outside.

Whenever Jane's mother arrived for one of her extended visits, strife was sure to follow. Ethel exerted undue influence over private family affairs, challenging my dad's role as head of the family. That they did not get along is an understatement, and the stress eventually tore the fabric of our family relationships.

Jane tried to stay neutral, but this was war—and I was at the epicenter. "There's going to be a divorce, and you are a big reason why," Ethel told me. "I hope you're happy."

After my dad filed for the divorce, I stayed in Hempstead for much of that summer. I got my learner's permit to drive and enjoyed a fleeting feeling of independence. I allowed myself to think that I might not have to go back to Harlingen. But that was not to be. My father pressured me, piling on layers of guilt and intimidation. Mimi was helpless to intervene, and so, reluctantly, I returned.

I was kept from Jane, Janet, or Meg for a long time after the divorce. My years of immersion in the Hack family dysfunctions had come to an end. We tried to stay in touch, but it was hard to muster the emotional energy. I had experienced very little that might be called family stability, and now I felt none.

Jane loved me in her way, and she did try to do the right things, but that relationship fell victim to the emotional crossfire between her mother and her husband. She knew that she should be loyal to him, but in the end, she could not deal with the stress from that conflict.

The marriage lacked affection and nurturing. My dad treated Jane condescendingly. He devalued and insulted her, and he didn't keep his attitude private. He expressed that disdain to his friends, too. He spoke of marriage with sarcasm and disrespect. It is no surprise that I grew up somewhat confused about what a healthy marriage and family life looked like. I knew what it *wasn't*. I just didn't know exactly what it *was*.

My dad demonstrated, again and again, that he cared more for himself than for me. Though I have forgiven him, I know that I must never justify his behavior. I can understand it without condoning it. He hurt me. Forgiving doesn't change that.

About a year after divorcing Jane, my father remarried and brought in *another* stepmother, Dorothy. He was determined that I accept her as my mother and treat her as such with deference and respect.

Having never married, Dorothy had an unfulfilled longing to become a wife and a mother. That desire aligned with my dad's motivation to re-create the happy family that was never going to be. That is what he had hoped Jane could do for him, but it was an impossible role for her. Now he pursued that same fantasy with Dorothy. I felt like an inanimate object—like a token on the gameboard.

It was during my summer stay in Hempstead, shortly after his remarriage, that I got word that I must come home early. He and Dorothy ushered me to the Cameron County Courthouse, where a magistrate recited something about my "legal disability" that I didn't understand. "Do you agree to this?" the judge asked.

"Yes?" I replied. It was clear that was the answer expected of me. Without consulting me, my father had obtained a legal document declaring that I was waiving my rights as a minor so that Dorothy could adopt me. She got herself a real live boy. We were now a "happy family" like a newly painted Norman Rockwell masterpiece.

As I saw it, Dorothy was just another woman my dad brought home so that I could have a mother. She soon demonstrated, though, that she was lacking in social skills. I came to realize later that she had a borderline personality disorder. In my eyes, she seemed crazy as a loon.

At every opportunity, Dorothy announced that I was her son. Even at age sixteen, I still was expected to play the role of the child—even so far as requiring me to hunt for Easter eggs. Nothing felt authentic about that time. This pretense of family was preposterous, and I was having no part of it. "*Oh Yeah? Watch This!*" I took defiance to a whole new level.

My father didn't understand what was wrong with me, nor with himself. For many years, throughout both his remarriages, this broken man still carried a color photograph of my mother in his wallet. By any other name, the woman he wanted was Mahalah Hamner Allen, and he was trying to get her back.

I didn't recognize at the time how this family brokenness was shaping my hopes, beliefs, and expectations about marriage and family. I resolved that if I married, I never would divorce, no matter what. Never. I believed that I would be able to "fix" any problem by just giving a little more. The years ahead would deliver a life lesson: some things would be just beyond my power to fix.

In 1989, when I was Captain of the aircraft carrier, *Coral Sea*, I received a call while at port in Norfolk. The message was tragic: My sister, Meg, who had struggled with breast cancer and depression, had passed. She left behind a loving husband and a precious little daughter. Meg's funeral was in Hinesville. I did not attend—not for lack of love or respect, but because I couldn't deal with the tension, shame, and guilt from the Hack family. I realize that my *not* attending could be judged as a defect of character, as a lack of courage to do the right thing.

Several years later, I visited Jane in Hinesville. She still had pictures of me along with Janet and Meg prominently displayed throughout the house. Jane always had honored Mahalah as my mother, and we shared a mutual affection and respect. When Jane died, I attended her funeral to honor her memory. Jane's daughter, Janet, lives in Boston now. We visit now and then—and every time, we pick up where we left off. She shares my sense of humor, and I have much love and affection for her. Together, so long ago, we endured pain and chaos that we could not understand. And in every visit, we come a little closer to making sense of it all. Some things cannot be fixed, but we can always work on the healing.

CHAPTER 4

MY DESTINY AS A NAVAL OFFICER

If I were to weigh the good memories of growing up in Harlingen against the bad ones, I'd rather focus on the former—the football games and Scout outings, the Sunday School lessons, and the afternoons with friends hunting rabbits and white-winged doves. I must not let the anguish of those years erase the fact that life had much to offer and that I anticipated a promising future. Until I left for college, though, I existed in a matrix of abuse and fear, evidenced by cysts and boils on my body. For much of third grade, I vomited before class.

Likewise, I must not overlook two strong values that my father instilled in me: the dignity and importance of hard work and the duty to care for the least among us. These principles were his gift to me. He valued education, and it was a given that I would go to college. Still, he saved my Tri-Pak union seniority number so that I would be able to return to my blue-collar job in the machine shop. My dad had little confidence that I would succeed. *"Oh Yeah? Watch This!"*

I was accepted into the University of Texas at Austin and graduated in four years with a bachelor's degree. I had internalized the message that I was "average" at best and that I was a C student. Indeed, I proved that I could make a C in any course, from literature to physics.

I did discover some leadership potential and served on the University of Texas Student Council. In my senior year, I was president of the Tejas Club, a non-Greek fraternity on campus that emphasizes scholarship and leadership. Its focus was on social and political affairs and other significant matters. I began to feel a sense of belonging and significance. I had a sense of destiny that I would realize in a way that I could never have imagined growing up.

Fly Air Force or Navy?

My intention after college was to pursue a graduate education. But I couldn't afford to go full-time, which was required for military deferment. The fact that I was about to be drafted certainly gave me a burst of patriotism—I wasn't going to leave this one to chance! The question wasn't whether I would enlist; it was which branch I would choose.

I ruled out the Army. Even my dad, who had been in the Army infantry two decades earlier in the Pacific, advised me to avoid any service that had the command, "Now fix bayonets!" So I applied to both the Navy and the Air Force and scored very high on aeronautical aptitude. Both branches wanted me to sign up. I couldn't decide which way to go.

Then I received a call from the Bergstrom Air Force Base Medical. Somehow the medics had lost all my lab work and requested that I retake part of my physical. That was it. I took the loss of my bodily fluids as a sign and decided to join the Navy—a decision that set the course for the rest of my life.

I often think about how what seems a normal decision can have profound consequences. Were it not for those lost vials, I might have joined the Air Force instead of the Navy. I was already a private pilot, but my less-than-perfect eyesight meant that I would qualify, not as a pilot but rather as an F-4 radar intercept officer (the character Goose in the movie *Top Gun*) or an A-6 bombardier navigator. In the Air Force at the time, this would have limited the opportunities for promotion or command—I could only expect to be promoted to Major or Lieutenant Colonel. The Navy, by contrast, recognized the critical role of Naval Flight Officers, especially bombardier-navigators in the A-6 Intruder and radar intercept officers in the F-4 Phantom. Without awareness, intention, or aspiration, I was destined to lead six Navy operational commands, two at the rank of Rear Admiral.

In November 1965, I commenced a sixteen-week Naval Aviation Officer Candidate program at the Naval Air Station in Pensacola, Florida. I put all my worldly possessions into my Volkswagen Beetle—stereo, rod and reel, shotgun in a secure case, a few changes of clothes, and a sports jacket—and arrived at the base on the weekend before Thanksgiving. I was due to report at ten o'clock on a Sunday night. My plan was to tour the Naval Air Station during daylight hours so that I'd know exactly where to report. Then there would be time to explore Pensacola and the beaches.

Let's take an inventory and do an assessment of my decisions to that point:

- planning to report early, tour the base, and locate the barracks where I would report: SMART
- planning to learn my way around Pensacola, especially the beaches: SMART

- failing to make further inquiries at the gate after the guard saw where I was headed, shook his head, put on a big smile, gave me some directions, waved me through, and said, knowingly, "Good luck": DUMB
- assuming I could "stop by" and just drop off my stuff: DUMB

I received a temporary vehicle pass, said "thanks" to the still-smiling gate guard, found my assigned building (a.k.a. World War II barracks), and parked in front. Up the stairs and through the entrance I went. Inside and to my left, I saw a cadet on duty behind a half-moon glass partition like the ones at a gas station in a bad neighborhood. Sliding my records through the glass opening, I said, "Hi, my name is Ed Allen, and I'll be back by 10 p.m. I'm going out to Pensacola Beach but wanted to make sure I could find this building after dark. Is there a place I can put my stuff, so I'll have it when I get back tonight?"

The cadet stared at me for a few seconds. His expression was a combination of surprise, condescension, disgust, and dark humor. He didn't say a word but simply pointed over the top of my left shoulder while making a stabbing motion with his finger.

I turned around and saw a Marine Corps Gunnery Sergeant. He was around 6-foot-4, weighed about 185 pounds, had about 8 percent body fat, and wore a perfect uniform. The shine on his shoes and belt buckle were high-noon bright, and he wore the USMC drill instructor campaign cover (a hat like the ones the Royal Canadian Mounted Police wear).

"You maggot!" he barked. "Your days of just strollin' into my building are over. I don't care if yo daddy is a United States senator, or yo mama is a movie star. You belong to *me* now, and I can't imagine how you could ever become an officer. Give me twenty pushups, and then run up and down that ladder [stairs] ten times. Right *now*."

Here's the censored version of what he said next: "There's a parking lot on the side of my building. You've got exactly three minutes to park that little girly car and get back here." I hustled to comply, and that was just the start of a memorable sixteen weeks.

Such was my introduction to becoming a naval aviation officer cadet. I soon learned that the big marine's name was Sergeant Montemayor. He later deployed to Vietnam. He did not return.

Courage and Determination

Those sixteen weeks of training were demanding, but most of the class graduated. The chief motivating factor was knowing that if you quit or flunked out, you were going to some ship in the fleet as a seaman (E-1) for two years and would be chipping paint, among other duties.

Morning reveille was played on a 45-rpm record at five o'clock throughout the battalion. I can still hear the scratchy noise of the needle hitting the record when I knew that I had about three more seconds before my feet had to hit the deck. We had morning formations along the sea plane ramps for inspections. I'll never forget standing there every morning with the wind blowing off the water, wearing only khaki trousers, a long-sleeved shirt, and a light Navy jacket. That was the coldest I can ever remember being in my life, even colder than Survival School in Brunswick, Maine, in February.

An important part of physical fitness training was to complete an obstacle course with a time limit: "No complete, off to the fleet." It was a reasonably demanding course, with all the typical obstacles, but the fact that it was in sand added to the difficulty.

One of those obstacles involved climbing a rope over a high wall and then crawling beneath a layer of wire. I had trouble getting over that wall. I wouldn't be physically qualified to be an officer unless I could complete the entire course in the allotted time. With only a couple of weeks before my last chance, I was highly motivated to conquer that wall. I practiced whenever I could on weekends until I learned the technique. Sitting at the top of the wall, I could see blue sky, white beaches, and other cadets marching off demerits. It was an exhilarating view. To those familiar with the course, it might not seem much of an achievement. For me, it was a glorious moment.

At graduation time, Mimi and my cousin, Gene, a U.S. Air Force (USAF) Colonel stationed at nearby Eglin Air Force Base (AFB), who had flown the "hump" during World War II, presented my commissioning ensign insignia. Back in 1945, Gene was the fifteen-year-old cousin who had come with my grandmother for my "authorized kidnapping" from Mimi and Papa Joe.

As a Naval Officer, a "Brown Bar" Ensign, I started to believe that I belonged. I had no intention of making the Navy a career, but I was acquiring an identity. A movie scene comes to mind from *An Officer and a Gentleman* in which Sgt. Foley (Lou Gossett Jr.) is taunting and daring Zack Mayo (Richard Gere) to quit Officer Candidate School. After being yelled at and humiliated, Zack screams, "No, sir. You can kick me outta' here, but I ain't quittin'. I got nowhere else to go." That was me. The Navy was becoming a family, where I was valued and respected—and just like Zack Mayo, I had nowhere else to go.

Next was Basic and Advanced Jet Training, which included flight planning, communications, navigation, plus air-air and air-ground weapons delivery. I realized that my flight spatial awareness, skills, and competencies were exceptional gifts. I received my Naval Flight Officer wings and orders to fly the F-4B Phantom.

Part of F-4 training was at the NAS Oceana in Virginia Beach, Virginia, and part at NAS Key West, Florida. In Florida, the weather was perfect almost year-round. We could take off with just a VFR clearance and quickly be in the restricted operating area. I learned day and night all-weather high-speed intercepts and air combat maneuvering. I recall zooming to 72K feet where the sky was dark blue—quiet and serene. There was one unique risk to night flying here. Looking down, you could see numerous fishing boats with white lights. Looking up, you saw only the lights from stars. So there were two fatal mishaps when similar lights above and below caused disorientation and loss of situational awareness.

The final F-4 training phase was day and night carrier qualifications (CarQuals). Ten daytime and six successful night landings over a period of at least two days were required to get a "complete." The second day landings went well, although the wind and seas were increasing and a low "scud layer" was forming. Night operations were on hold until the Captain and Landing Signal Officer could assess the weather.

We finally received the "launch 'em!" order. We completed the remaining required night landings, and they were "colorful." The weather was low overcast, limited visibility, and the deck was moving; flight operations were canceled after our last landing. Back in the Ready Room, I remember commenting on the level of difficulty getting aboard—I had assumed this was just "ops normal." The Officer in Charge asked me who I was flying with. I told him, and he started laughing. It seems our last two landings were nearly ramp strikes. The pilot I was with turned in his wings, meaning "I quit." I didn't know any better and had apparently underestimated the level of difficulty this particular night.

Having completed F-4 training, I reported to Fighter Squadron VF-41, the "Black Aces," to fulfill my 1967–1970 three-year contract. We made two nine-month deployments with the Sixth Fleet in the

Mediterranean: one in the USS *Independence* (CV-62) and the other in USS *Franklin D. Roosevelt* (CV-42).

For the *Roosevelt* deployment, we were ordered for a transit to the Pacific Seventh Fleet for Vietnam combat operations. I thought I would finally see real combat. But the bombing was halted, and we returned to another tour with the Sixth Fleet. I would deploy to Vietnam but not until the end of the war for the evacuation of Saigon.

Little did I realize that eighteen years later, I would command the USS *Coral Sea* (CV-43), a Midway-class carrier like the USS *Franklin D. Roosevelt*. The USS *Independence* was part of Carrier Group Four (CCG-4). Twenty-two years later, I would command that Carrier Group Four as a Rear Admiral.

There is a theme of my life of always seeking to become stronger, better informed, well-read, and to make the most of what intellectual capacity I had been given. God had given me enough talent to do well, but I had to work hard to "do well." During the months ashore, I undertook two ways to improve. First, I enrolled in the Evelyn Wood speed reading course. The class met weekly for six weeks with an hour of practice six days a week. I was diligent in the practice and developed my reading speed and comprehension significantly. I have the versatile skills to read both short articles and lengthy books at a fast pace. As one's speed increases, so does comprehension. I also completed the Dale Carnegie course to develop my public speaking and interpersonal skills.

I had many memorable day and night sorties off the carrier and unique training exercises with French fighters. We had port calls and liberty ashore in Mediterranean ports such as Rota, Spain, Palma de Mallorca; Marseilles, France; Naples, Italy; Istanbul, Turkey; and Haifa, Israel.

It was during this tour that I started my quest to become an authentic leader, and that quest continues to this day. I was an ensign, and my first lesson was to listen to the chief petty officer assigned to my division. His real responsibility was my professional development.

Leadership at the "deck plate" level (main deck on a carrier) was somewhat more "personalized" than today. One day the chief, who looked like Lou Gossett in *An Officer and a Gentleman*, told me that an airman named Morelli had an attitude problem and asked me what he should do about it.

"Why don't you just counsel him, Chief?" I said.

He grinned mischievously. "Aye, aye, sir."

I saw Morelli the next day on the flight deck as we were manning up our Phantom. Morelli was moving slowly and walking with a slight limp. Upon return from my flight, I asked the chief what had happened to Morelli.

"Ensign, you told me to counsel Morelli," he said, smiling. "Well, I counseled him. I counseled him *real good.*"

In August 1969, my three-year Navy contract was nearly up. We were not shown our performance evaluations (called "fitness reports"), but I learned later that I had done well and was considered to have strong career potential.

I got a call one day from a Navy personnel assignment officer in Washington. "Ed, what are you going to do next?"

"What do you mean, what am I going to do next?" I replied. "I'm going home to Texas for graduate education."

"OK, here's the deal," he said. "You can extend your contract for two years for orders to the Naval ROTC unit in Austin as an assistant professor of naval science. Let us know what you would like to do."

If I accepted, I could stay on active duty. I would be a member of the faculty and get Longhorn football tickets and reserved parking place. I could also attend graduate school. I accepted the offer for a two-year extension of my Navy contract.

But there was a problem. The University of Texas Faculty Committee rejected my nomination. My academic record did not meet the requirements of assistant professor status. No surprise there. I wasn't exactly Mensa Society material, but I was better than a C student, my transcript notwithstanding.

I took leave and flew to Austin at my own expense to meet with the UT ROTC Commander to plead my case. After an extended interview, he said, "Thanks for stopping by, I'll be in touch."

The Captain met with the faculty committee and presented my case based on my Navy record and my "tenacity of spirit." In a couple of weeks, I received a call saying that indeed I was accepted. It was yet one more time that I'd proceeded with an attitude of "*Oh Yeah? Watch This!*" I was getting the distinct impression that somebody was truly watching.

CHAPTER 5

FROM ACADEMIA TO F-14A TOMCATS

It was 1970, and it had been four years since I was last on campus at the University of Texas. I found the atmosphere to be much different. I was in uniform now, an Assistant Professor of Naval Science. The anti-war movement was boiling over. Occasionally, I was harassed and insulted while in uniform, though student opposition in Austin wasn't as intense as at other universities, such as Berkeley.

My duties as the sophomore instructor included educating third-class midshipmen in naval history and strategy and to give training on military rules, regulations, rank structure, and Navy organization. That left me with sufficient time to pursue graduate work. My first course was a graduate seminar with Dr. Walt Rostow, who had been President Lyndon Johnson's national security advisor and then came to Texas to teach and oversee the LBJ Library.

Dr. Rostow was an architect of the Vietnam strategy and clearly a hawk. His course was titled "What Alternatives Were Possible for the Vietnam Conflict Other Than the One Pursued, and Why Would This Alternative Have Been More Successful?" He had a strong positive bias toward the military and wanted to know our views on the war, challenging us to the extreme. He was patient with me, listening to my ideas with sincere interest. Try as I might, I could not agree with his "gradualism" warfighting strategy, though I recognized his brilliance.

As the semester began, I attended a reception for new faculty members, wearing my "choker whites" dress uniform. There I met Linda Bley, an Assistant Professor of Foods And Nutrition. She was Irish, very attractive, smart, and spirited. We dated for several months and were married the following year in the University Methodist Church near the campus.

Our intentions were to stay in Austin while I completed my Navy contract, and Linda continued teaching and working on her PhD in foods and nutrition. I had no specific goals other than to complete graduate school and go into business.

In the summer, I had two groups of third-class midshipmen that spent four weeks each at the Naval Air Station Corpus Christi for orientation in naval aviation. They participated in physical fitness, swimming training, sports, rifle range, and aviation basics with orientation flights. I was the officer who managed their training. The routine allowed plenty of time for Linda and me to enjoy the summer, socializing and enjoying the beaches. I bought a big motorcycle, and we took many delightful rides along the Texas coast.

Another Offer I Couldn't Refuse

At the end of two years at Austin, I attained a master's degree with a thesis on the emerging Soviet Navy, and in the spring of 1972, we started making transition plans from the academic to the civilian world. Then the Navy made another offer I couldn't refuse. The new F-14 Tomcat fighter was being introduced into the fleet, and a small cadre of pilots and radar intercept officers was selected to establish the first two squadrons.

The reputation of Navy fighter aviators appealed to both of us. This was an opportunity to live in San Diego, where I would be stationed at "Fighter Town," Naval Air Station Miramar. I extended my Navy Reserve contract for two years, and we moved to San Diego. We bought a home near the beach in Encinitas and decided there was just no finer year-round weather than the Southern California coast. Our social life included squadron events, tennis, sports events, horse races at the Del Mar racetrack, and dining at places like the well-known Bully's in Del Mar.

It was an exciting, high-energy environment, and we had no obligations except each other and our dog, Razzle Dazzle, a Basenji we bought while still on campus. As a breed, Basenjis are smart, quiet, energetic, and fearless. They also are highly spirited, with stubborn and defiant traits—and that also would describe Linda and me during this time.

The two of us shared an adventurous spirit and were motivated to achieve something special. Unfortunately, I had a family background with some dysfunction. I didn't know what a healthy family looked like and didn't have the emotional maturity to establish one. Both of us expected that the other would provide the love and strength needed for a successful marriage. Neither of us could do that.

Looking back, our time in San Diego was the best of our marriage. It was also the beginning of a long story that did not end well. We looked good on the outside but not on the inside. Our marriage would not survive.

Tactics and Carrier Operations at Sea

In October 1972, the first two F-14 squadrons (the VF-1 Wolfpack and VF-2 Bounty Hunters) were commissioned with new F-14s at Miramar. We spent the next twenty months developing new fighter tactics and focusing on air combat maneuvering. We fired live missiles against drones that simulated actual MIG flight profiles. We fired guns against towed banners. We also had air combat training with Air Force fighters.

In the final phase, we prepared for the first operational deployment to the Western Pacific and Indian Ocean off the USS *Enterprise* (CVN-65). We trained for day and night carrier operations.

No one had focused on how the F-14 would be integrated into the Battle Group weapons systems. So I started looking more at *strategy* than *tactics*. How would the new fighters operate with other Carriers and Air Wings and Battle Groups, including air, surface and submarine platforms, weapons systems, and weapons with a wide range of warfighting capabilities?

I proposed formation of an F-14 Fleet Tactics Team, and the Commanding Office approved my proposal. He also approved my attendance to the Navy Tactical Action Officer school. There I studied Navy fleet-level tactics and focused on integrating the F-14A as a weapons system with current fleet ships sensors and weapons.

Every ship has a Tactical Action Officer (TAO) trained in naval tactics, ships' weapons, sensors and systems, and how to win against air, surface, submarine, or electronic threats. It is a complex responsibility. At the completion of TAO school, I proposed formation of a small group to develop integrated fleet tactics and write a Fleet Air Superiority Manual. When the initial work was complete, the Commanding Officer scheduled briefings for Two- and Three Star Admirals and their staffs reporting our progress to date.

MCNAMARA'S "FLYING EDSEL"

There is an interesting story behind the F-14 becoming the new Navy fighter. In the early 1960s, both the Navy and the Air Force needed a combat aircraft. The Navy needed a carrier-based fighter for fleet defense and a dogfighter with a gun. The Air Force needed a supersonic, low-level fighter bomber that could avoid detection by enemy radar and avoid surface-to-air missiles.

Traditionally, each service developed its own aircraft to meet its service requirements. Secretary of Defense McNamara determined that millions could be saved with a common airframe, the two very different missions notwithstanding. Neither service believed that the result met their service requirements. The F-111 was developed for the Air Force, and a Navy version, the F-111B, became known as the "flying Edsel."

A core requirement of the Navy version was the ability to carry the new long-range F-111B's Phoenix missile, and the Navy had no alternative for a fighter version. In 1967, Grumman proposed an alternative design based on Navy requirements for a swing-wing fighter capable of both carrying the Phoenix and dogfighting—thus, the F-14 Tomcat.

Vice Admiral Tom Connolly testified before the Senate Armed Services Committee and was asked if the F-111B new engines would meet carrier operation requirements. Vice Admiral Connolly stated, "Senator, there isn't enough thrust in all of Christendom to make that airplane suitable." That was the end of the Navy F-111B and Vice Admiral Connolly's career. That part of his testimony had not been cleared by the Navy.

On the First F-14 Deployment

I recall standing at the ship's railing as the USS *Enterprise* took in all lines to steam under the Golden Gate Bridge and head for the Western Pacific and Indian Ocean for eight months. I spotted Linda down among the crowd, looking up at me. I can see her even now as she appeared that day, standing on the pier in her light-colored suit. All around her, the loved ones of others on the ship were waving exuberantly. I waved to her. She moved her hand slightly, almost imperceptibly, to signal her farewell.

This was September 1974. It was the first deployment for the F-14, a high-visibility, high-energy, high-recognition, and somewhat higher-risk operation. Everything we did was a "first-time" event. Although any port call is a highly visible event, there was even more publicity with the USS *Enterprise* (CVN-65) being nuclear-powered and carrying the new F-14A fighters.

We represented the power and diplomacy of the United States. Our Ports of Call included Pearl Harbor, the Philippine Islands, Hong Kong, Singapore, and Mombasa, Kenya. The Battle Group Commander and Captain paid formal calls on the governor and local leaders and hosted reciprocal VIP ship visits with a Sunset Parade on the Flight Deck or Hangar Deck.

This was also a time of liberty for the crew, with numerous social events and tours to local cultural and historical sites. There were community-support events where groups of the crew would volunteer to support projects like repairing local homes, schools, churches, and working with other community groups. This enabled us to represent the United States as goodwill ambassadors and for our sailors to experience other cultures.

We conducted day and night flight operations and fleet training exercises with our Battle Group and with our allies, the most noteworthy being with the French carrier *Clemenceau*.

We also experienced a major engine problem with the F-14 TF-30 engine. Compressor blades fractured and destroyed electrical and hydraulic systems on two aircraft. The event was described as a "thump bang," and the aircraft was immediately uncontrollable. Fortunately, four successful Martin-Baker ejection seats worked as advertised, and all four aviators were rescued and returned to flying status. The F-14s were grounded for several weeks until the cause was determined and modifications made. As a temporary fix, compressor blades were strengthened and engine protective casings modified.

The fact that Navy engineers and technicians were able to determine the cause and make engine modifications while the F-14's were forward deployed on a carrier is a tribute to naval aviation engineering. We resumed flight operations with some temporary flight maneuvering restrictions.

Soon after the *Enterprise* departed from our port call in Mombasa, a cyclone hit the island of Mauritius. Water supplies were contaminated, thousands of homes destroyed, power and communications cut off, and roads blocked. The *Enterprise* turned southeast and steamed more than 1,600 miles around the northern coast of Madagascar to Port Louis, Mauritius.

Several hundred of the *Enterprise* crew were organized into work parties and provided disaster relief for four long days, surveying damage to sugarcane fields, supplying 60,000 gallons of fresh water, and repairing storm damage to buildings. *Enterprise* doctors and corpsmen provided medical care to hospitals and orphanages. Roads were cleared, power lines repaired, and airport navigation aids and facilities were repaired.

In early April we departed for home, as the Vietnam War was drawing to a close. After a few days steaming east, we were turned around and proceeded back to the coast of Vietnam to fly fighter-cover for the evacuation of the U.S. Embassy in Saigon. The operation on April 30, 1975, became known as Operation Frequent Wind. It was a historic event for the first F-14A "combat" sorties as we flew air cover during the evacuation.

You might recall the classic photograph of the Air America helicopter on a Saigon rooftop with American civilians and "at-risk" Vietnamese climbing makeshift ladders to be evacuated, some hanging from the helicopter skids. In desperation, some of them were fleeing in small aircraft, purposefully crashing into the water next to the carriers to be rescued.

The last U.S. helicopter departed Saigon, and President Duong Van Minh surrendered unconditionally. The Communist forces renamed the capital Ho Chi Minh City, although the ancient city still is often called Saigon both locally and internationally.

In May of that year, we stopped at Pearl Harbor, Hawaii, for some well-earned liberty and to commence the USS *Enterprise* "Tiger Cruise." One hundred fifty sons of the ship/Air Wing and several sons of Vietnam POWs or missing in action (MIAs) ages eight to eighteen sailed with us during the five-day transit to San Francisco. They experienced life at sea and observed Carrier and Air Wing operations. They toured the ship and heard lectures at the various departments, such as Navigation, Flight Operations, Deck Seamanship, Engineering, Weapons, Communications, and Air Wing Aircraft. They observed the catapult launch of the Air Wing to fly enroute to their home bases. Then *Enterprise* sailed under the Golden Gate Bridge into San Francisco Bay and dockside at Naval Air Station Alameda.

Flash forward about fifteen years to when I was Commanding Officer of the USS *Coral Sea*. We had stopped in Halifax, Nova Scotia, for a Tiger Cruise to Norfolk. At the dinner table, our daughter Ashley spoke up, "Hey, Dad, you say I can be anything I want to be—so why, as a girl, can't I take part in this Tiger Cruise?" Remember, this was 1990, and no women were serving on ships or in combat billets. I didn't have an immediate answer for Ashley, but I took her seriously. I managed to overcome resistance and obtain authorization, and we developed a detailed plan for embarking both men and women—and we all enjoyed a memorable Tiger-Tigress cruise. This was a significant event for the Navy, although I suspect John Paul Jones would not have approved.

My Marriage Strength Fading

My Navy performance continued to excel, but my marriage did not. Linda and I had not agreed on the nature and demands of Navy life, especially the long months of extended deployments, family separation, and the life of a Navy wife. This meant understanding that I could not return during deployment except for critical emergencies and then only if operational commitments permitted. Communication would be limited to mid-'70s technology. Snail mail was the primary means of communicating, and a letter could take a few weeks to nearly a month. Phone calls were limited and cost $13 a minute.

Linda was a strong and independent woman with her own identity and career. She resented setting aside her personal and professional lives and being defined in the role of a Navy wife. "I didn't sign up for this," she often told me. She was correct.

And she had not expected to be left behind and alone. I often thought back on that day when I waved to her from the railing of the *Enterprise*. She looked lost, confused, and forlorn. It was as if my departure had triggered a long-standing fear of abandonment. At the time, I believed that I could "fix it" and that we could make it work, but she didn't have the confidence to go it alone. Our relationship was never the same after that.

CHAPTER 6

ASPIRATIONS AND TENSIONS

We are smiling and laughing as Linda joins me at the foot of a California ski slope. She seems happy, and we are together. It is a moment frozen in time, but even as I recall that weekend in the California mountains, other moments invade my memories. I hear crying, faintly at first, then louder.

This was May 1975, not long after I had returned to San Diego from deployment on the *Enterprise* and rejoined Linda in our home in nearby Del Mar. We were going through the motions of making our marriage work, but the good times by then were only occasional.

A period of adjustment is normal after a long deployment, but this was more than that. We were changing. Our sense of "we" was fading. Rather than celebrating our reunion and delighting in our relationship, we were trying to recapture it. We both sensed the strain. A bright light for Linda was her appointment to teach foods and nutrition at San Diego State University. I was consumed and totally

57

focused on flying and the anticipation of the first F-14 deployment. The energy and joy of our first months in San Diego were gone.

I soon was assigned the responsibility of squadron safety officer, a duty that required completion of the Naval Aviation Safety Course at the Navy Postgraduate School at Monterey, California. Meanwhile, the demanding schedule of the squadron turnaround training cycle continued.

Aide to Vice Admiral, Head of Naval Aviation ... in the Pentagon

In June 1976, about a year after returning to San Diego, I received orders to report to the Pentagon. I was to be the Aide and Administrative Assistant to the Three Star Vice Admiral responsible for all naval aviation programs, including aircraft carriers, aircraft, and weapons systems. This was a visible and sensitive position, a key support role to the highest level of decision-making in naval aviation. I didn't make decisions, but I was in the arena. Professionally, this was the best assignment for me.

I was excited. Linda was not. Nevertheless, we were off to the East Coast. Linda resigned from her teaching position. We sold our home in Del Mar, and that for a while boosted her spirits. Soon we were living in Springfield, Virginia—cold winters, hot summers, long working hours, congested traffic, and higher cost of living.

I hadn't really talked to Linda about whether moving across the country was what she wanted. We didn't make a joint decision and commit to it. I made the decision, and she complied, reluctantly. I presumed that the move would be no big deal. It was a very big deal. Linda tried to adapt, but she had no friends, no family nearby, no opportunity to teach. And she was pregnant with Ashley.

In my assignment at the Pentagon, I was responsible for the Admiral's schedule, all correspondence, monitoring phone calls, and staying current on issues, pending decisions, and flag-level interaction. I scheduled all travel, coordinating each visit and following up on actions, decisions, and commitments. I was privy to calls with congressmen and senators as well as congressional testimony.

Military and social events filled many evenings. I was present at the commissioning of the USS *Nimitz* (CVN-68) and events like the Paris Air Show. Linda and I attended the Presidential Inauguration and ball for Jimmy Carter. We attended the U.S. Marine Corps Sunset Parade, a special display of pride and gratitude.

In short, I experienced in those two years a period of strong professional satisfaction. I was also spending long hours working and commuting. Nevertheless, I was working with the top leaders in naval aviation and becoming well known.

Ashley's birth was a joy that deepened my appreciation of God's blessings. Never will I forget how it felt to hold her for the first time. My career obligations kept me busy, but I made the effort to be involved and engaged in being a new dad. I would rise at five o'clock in the morning, jog three miles, and then return to spend some time with her—even if it was changing her diaper and feeding her a bottle—before heading off to the Pentagon.

I think back on that time, and I see another scene, so vividly: I am a young man in uniform, holding his newborn daughter. With a finger against her cheek, I close my eyes and begin humming and then softly singing: "Jesus loves me, this I know" and "Rock a bye baby."

As the months passed, Linda consistently declined to accept invitations to functions for Navy wives. As a couple, we found ourselves no longer included in social activities other than formal events. The stress and unhappiness were palpable.

Somehow, I believed I could repair this brokenness, this conflict between career and marriage. And if I had doubts, I declared to myself, *"Oh Yeah? Watch This!"* It was my old attitude that had served me well in the past. This time, that strategy didn't work. But what were my choices, separation or divorce; never! Recall my vow to never be divorced.

Back to Miramar

In the spring of 1978, I received orders to return to Miramar as the operations officer of a Carrier Air Wing. I had earned a solid professional reputation, and this was another challenging assignment. Linda and I and Ashley bought a townhouse in Del Mar, and it was back to squadron life.

A Naval Aviation Carrier Air Wing is composed of different types of aircraft and different missions. As the operations officer, I could fly in the F-14 Tomcat, the A-6E Intruder, EA-6B Prowler, the E-2C Hawkeye, S-3A Viking, and SH-3 Sea King. Working closely with the squadron Commanding Officers, I learned the capabilities of those aircraft and many valuable lessons. I represented or spoke on behalf of the Air Wing Commander, carrier Captain, and the Battle Group Commander and his staff. The experience prepared me for success when I became an air wing Commander five years later.

Normally an Air Wing and Carrier are located on the same coast. We had the additional challenge of being a West Coast Air Wing and deploying in the USS *America* (CV-66) on the East Coast. Though we were home-based on the West Coast, we would be doing integrated training in the Puerto Rican Operating Area. That required unique planning and training.

Then came our seven-month deployment to the Sixth Fleet, operating and training in the Mediterranean. During our many port calls, we had the opportunity to enjoy a variety of cultures in the region as representatives of the United States. At the end of deployment, we headed west though the Straits of Gibraltar to the East Coast of the United States. We launched the Air Wing, and the squadrons returned to their respective Naval Air Stations at North Island, Miramar, Lemoore, and Whidbey Island.

During much of that deployment, which lasted into 1979, I did not see much of Linda and Ashley, though they did come to Europe during our port call in Naples, and we enjoyed a short but memorable vacation to Rome, Florence, and Spain. Linda seemed happier now, having resumed teaching. Ashley had started preschool. Together finally in San Diego, the three of us had the opportunity to function as a family.

CHAPTER 7

WINNING IS MORE THAN "NOT LOSING"

Sitting on the dais in my full dress whites with sword, I looked out over the 150 guests at the Change of Command ceremony. There, in the front row, were Linda and Ashley, and with them was my dad, full of pride. It was June 1980, and I had been selected to assume Command of F-14 Fighter Squadron One (VF-1). For sixteen months, I would be Executive Officer, after which I would assume Command of the Squadron for fifteen months. This was my first opportunity for Command at Sea, the ultimate goal of a Naval Officer and an opportunity for complete authority, responsibility, and accountability.

The ceremony was on the parade grounds of "Fightertown USA," at the Naval Air Station Miramar. On the dais with me were the Air Wing Commander, the outgoing Commanding Officer, the Chaplain, and the Adjutant, all in full dress whites. After the parading of the colors, the invocation, and the Commanding Officer's departing remarks, I assumed command with the words, "I relieve you, sir." I was now the skipper of VF-1.

In my remarks, I reminded all of us that Navy carrier aviation was a special calling with a proud heritage—in the battles of Coral Sea, Midway, and Leyte Gulf and in the valiant flying in the Korean War and in the skies over Vietnam by Navy and Marine Corps heroes. After a reception at the Officer's Club, Linda and I hosted a spirited squadron party that evening at our home in Del Mar.

I didn't want that fabulous Friday to be over, but it was followed by reality Monday.

Command Leadership

My role as Executive Officer prior to assuming Command was to lead through influence, setting the example in the air, at sea, and ashore. I emphasized leadership, professional development, and recognition for the crew.

Much of my time I spent teaching and mentoring each officer, one on one. I studied them—their personalities, strengths, challenges, and potential. I witnessed how they would operate under both normal and stressful conditions. I got an idea of their principles and values. And I saw whether they were team players, which was essential to our success.

The plain truth was that we had only one way to go—up. The twelve F-14 fighter squadrons at Miramar were ranked frequently based on key performance indicators. VF-1 was ranked toward the bottom. We needed bold, decisive change, and I intended to deliver it.

On that first Monday morning, I had prepared for my initial all-officers meeting in the Ready Room.[1] There was greatness there. These were men who knew how to win, but not many of them had experienced what it means to be the best.

Entering the room at nine o'clock sharp, I stood erect next to the podium. I made eye contact with every officer before I spoke a word. "We fight to win," I began, "but right now we have a 'not losing' attitude." I'm no Bear Bryant or Vince Lombardi, but for the next hour, I spoke with confidence, clarity, and intensity. I left no doubt about our standards, boundaries, what they could expect of me, and what I would expect of them.

So how do you go about rebuilding a team? We needed to commit to a vision, and it had to be compelling and challenging. I had a clear picture of the powerful, professional team that we would become, in fierce pursuit of excellence, and what that would look like when we got there.

You can't get anywhere, though, unless you get started—and first impressions matter. We needed to be diligent about our appearance— the Ready Room, hangar deck, flight deck, maintenance control, anything, and everything that would signal our devotion to excellence. We needed to look sharp in uniform, carrying ourselves with purpose and confidence. We needed to look like more than winners. We needed to look like champions.

In the Navy, you often hear the adage of "a place for everything and everything in its place." To leave a lasting impression, our work-

---

1   The Ready Room is a dedicated squadron space on the carrier and ashore. The Ready Room has armchair seats with fold-up table tops for the Commanding Officer and the executive officer and the other officers assigned by rank. An aircraft tracking board shows aircraft status, crew members, and mission type. This is also a space where aircrews can hold informal meetings. Movies were shown in the evenings after flight ops were completed.

spaces at Miramar and on the ship had to be clean, well-lighted, and well-organized, with tools, equipment, and supplies in their proper place. "I've seen some clean ships that couldn't shoot," an Admiral once said, "but I've never seen a dirty one that could."

Our aircrafts were clean, yes—clean enough. The squadron spaces were reasonably organized but nothing special—just satisfactory. The aircrews flew "intelligently aggressive" and won most of the time. The briefs and debriefs were professional and focused on lessons learned and improving our tactics. We had no lack of talent and motivation. What our squadron's current culture lacked was the sense of urgency that would refuse to accept *winning as not losing*.

Two squadrons can have the same aircraft, the same schedule, the same levels of manning, funding, and support but still be dramatically different in their readiness and performance. The leadership is what makes the difference. In striving to build a champion team, I vowed to start with myself. What I expected of others was what I expected of myself, and if I made a bad call, I would admit to being wrong. I promised the team that we would be clear about our vision and how we would reach it and that would mean committing to long days of hard training, doing whatever it would take. I committed to the professional development and growth of every officer. We would settle for nothing but the best.

This was a particularly challenging goal in the late 1970s and early 1980s, which were tough times for military readiness, especially for the Navy. Reduced defense spending in the Carter administration negatively impacted training, flight hours, and the ability to maintain sufficient readiness. All squadrons operated with minimum flight hours per month and with little support in parts and repair capabilities. This started to turn around when President Reagan assumed office in January 1981, and within a few months, we began to benefit from his leadership and a significant increase in funding.

We were at the beginning of our Turnaround Training plan, and our focus was on individual and squadron readiness. Then we began training as an Airwing, with complex mission exercises like large attack and fighter missions, antisubmarine warfare, and electronic warfare. The final phase of intensive training involved integrating the airwing with the carrier and getting ready for deployment. This meant day and night at-sea operations, culminating in a seventy-two-hour around-the-clock simulation of actual combat.

Success breeds success. Our squadron got better and better in the game of air superiority in any arena. Once low ranked, VF-1 now received the highest grades possible for a fighter squadron. Certified for deployment, we continued to perform in the Persian Gulf—and upon completion of my command tour, I received my next orders.

National War College Class of 1983

After my fighter squadron command, I was selected for the 1983 National War College class at Ft. Leslie J. McNair in Washington, District of Columbia. The National War College is a ten-month program of study for senior military officers from all the services as well as civilian decision-makers from the Department of State, Central Intelligence Agency (CIA), Federal Bureau of Investigation (FBI), Defense Intelligence Agency (DIA), and other agencies. The goal was to educate future military and civilian leaders on national security strategies and decision-making for executing high-level policy.

Ft. McNair is near the White House, the Supreme Court, and Congress, which enables a distinguished collection of guest speakers.

Our class heard from the attorney general, the national security advisor, and senators.

The National War College emphasized wellness and fitness and included several intramural sports competitions. As part of my commitment to fitness, I took up jogging. My first race was the Marine Corps Marathon with Jack Ensch. My time was of four hours fifteen minutes. I knew that I was capable of a sub four-hour time, so I ran the marathon again the following year, in freezing cold with sleet. We were given space blankets along the way, and several participants had to drop out. I was proud to just finish in four hours and thirty minutes, which was slower than the previous year.

After War College graduation, I reported to the Navy staff in the Pentagon, awaiting orders to San Diego for command of a Carrier Air Wing—the first of what I call the three "mountaintop experiences."

CHAPTER 8

COMMAND AT SEA

After War College graduation, I reported to the Navy staff in the Pentagon, awaiting command of an Air Wing in Miramar. All three of us looked forward to returning to San Diego. Linda would resume her teaching at San Diego State, and Ashley could start first grade. Ashley made some lifelong friends and developed a love of the California lifestyle.

Command of a Carrier Air Wing (CAG) was the first of three "mountaintop" experiences in my professional life. The "mountaintop" was more than successful achievement of a goal. It was a challenge of great responsibility, clear purpose, powerful goals, and fierce commitment to winning. When on the mountaintop, I was living my purpose and was "in the zone."

I felt that I was made for this assignment—I was where I was supposed to be, doing what I was supposed to be doing. This was a challenge with clear purpose that I executed with fierce commitment. Every day, I felt full of energy and confidence as I relentlessly attended to the duties of leadership. It felt natural. I was "in the zone."

Since all eight of the squadron Commanding Officers were in San Diego for the change of command ceremony, I scheduled a two-day conference to develop our training plan for the next deployment. I prepared carefully and thoroughly, as I had only one shot to make that first impression.

I focused that conference on leadership and professional development from a perspective of "what do followers expect of leaders?" The priorities were integrity, professional competence, and a clear vision. I had the first two, and I also had a good idea of what our vision should be—but I needed to communicate it clearly to these officers and make it *ours*, not just mine. So, after all, they would be living that vision. By collaborating on creating it, they would own it.

Before assuming command of the Air Wing, I spent five months learning the capabilities and limitations of each type of aircraft. I requalified in the F-14 and then qualified as an A-6E Bombardier/ Navigator (B/N) syllabus at NAS Whidbey Island in Washington. My top priority was to understand strike planning and execution. I also trained on the EA-6B Prowler Electronic Warfare capabilities at Whidbey Island. I then focused on the E-2C, home-based at Miramar, and the S-3A Viking and SH-3 at North Island, California. The training and familiarization flights built my knowledge and competency with each of the aircraft.

One of those flights, in the SH-3 helicopter, was particularly memorable. Three of us—the pilot, aircrewman, and I flew from NAS North Island out over the desert and mountainous terrain to 29 Palms Training Area, north of Palm Springs. After training there, we were returning to San Diego by the same route, and I had the controls. It was almost sunset. We passed over Palm Springs and started our ascent to clear the mountains.

I routinely asked the pilot whether all systems were OK. He scanned the instruments, and his response was abrupt: "I've got the controls." The main rotor was losing oil pressure. Not good. We needed to land as soon as possible and headed back over Palm Springs.

I spotted a Walmart parking lot. "How about setting down there?" I asked. The pilot pointed instead to a golf course where one of the greens was clear, and we landed safely at dusk on Hole #8 at the Morningside Golf Course, where a curious crowd of golfers and nearby homeowners gathered. Squadron maintenance personnel soon came in to repair the helicopter, and a new crew flew it out the next day. It all happened without interfering with golf course operations. We wouldn't have wanted to get in the way of President Ford, after all. Or Jack Nicklaus.

Turnaround Training

Turnround training is executed in three phases. In the first phase, the squadrons train as individual units. They operate from their respective home bases and with specific type of training. The fighter squadrons, therefore, deployed to Naval Air Facility (NAF) El Centro, California, for the Fleet Fight Air Combat Readiness Program (FFACRP). (We were world class in acronyms!) The S-3 squadron deployed to Hawaii for antisubmarine training.

I traveled to all the squadrons' detachment training. My schedule would allow only one day in Hawaii for S-3A, but just showing up and being present were significant.

In the second phase, we train as an Air Wing. We integrate all the eight squadrons to operate as one unit. Together we deployed to the Fallon Range Training Complex (FRTC) in western Nevada. We trained on ranges and targets with live ordnance, executing coordinated strikes, day and night; fighter training against multiple targets simulating actual opponents; and electronic warfare training against fixed and mobile threats. We conducted aerial refueling and actual combat search and rescue (CSAR) training. We evaluated our tactics for real-world execution.

We tested and evaluated the contingency plans we might need during our extended deployment to the Western Pacific and Indian Ocean. One contingency plan was to execute a surprise attack deep inside a target country. I'll not include operational details, but the plan was for some aircraft to ingress at night, at low level through the mountains. This was a high-risk tactic and was one of my toughest decisions as a CAG because this sortie was not required. It was the idea of the squadron Commanding Officers, and I approved it. Was the increased higher probability of mission success worth the increased risk of aircraft losses? I believed that the training versus the risk was the right thing to do. Just prior to Fallon, I tasked the best F-14 crew and the best A-6 crew to evaluate the tactic by flying a similar route in the Cascade Mountains. They flew the route in daytime and then the same route at night. These flights would be opposed by simulated enemy flying a threat profile.

I had to decide whether our training for this scenario merited the risk. I considered the pros and cons. First, the pros: this was a real-world contingency with significant consequences, good or bad. We had seasoned A-6 and F-14 aircrews, and I trusted my leadership as well as the Commanding Officers and the flight leads. We could fairly and professionally evaluate the probability of success.

As for the cons, my career was at stake if this didn't go well. I would be judged and held accountable for a bad decision. It would mean I would not be getting the command of a ship or aircraft carrier, and I certainly would not be promoted to Admiral. I had everything to lose and nothing to gain except establishing that the mission was possible, significant insofar as it might provide a real-world option.

We completed all the Fallon training successfully. By the time we departed Fallon, we knew the strengths that we could build upon and the weaknesses to correct. We had built a team—and now it was "show time," when we would integrate the Air Wing and the aircraft carrier. We would fight as one team on any mission, day or night, in any weather.

I left the Air Wing just before an extended deployment by USS *Ranger* (CV-61). My departing thought was that I had been entrusted with a powerful Air Wing capable of keeping the peace and prepared, if required, to inflict violent destruction. At the same time, I was responsible for the safety and security of 1,500 of our nation's officers and sailors devoted to defending our country. My role was to lead, train, and inspire that team to be combat ready for any contingency. All of us simply did our duty.

Captain of the USS *Vancouver* (LPD-2)

Command of an aircraft carrier requires years of carrier aviation experience, successful command of a carrier-based squadron, and command of a replenishment ship or amphibious assault ship, a "deep draft." At this point, I had completed seven extended carrier deployments, including command of a carrier-based fighter squadron, and was qualified as a Surface Warfare Officer and as a Command Duty Officer USS. Command of the USS *Vancouver* (LPD-2) fulfilled the "deep draft" prerequisite for carrier command.

I completed seven months of specialized training at four different locations before assuming command of the *Vancouver*, which was deployed in the Western Pacific. The ship was an Austin Class with a "landing platform dock." She was 522 feet long, capable of 21 knots top speed, and could carry more than a thousand sailors and Marines. She had a flight deck, a well deck, and ballast system to launch and recover amphibious boats. The *Vancouver* also could embark air cushion (LCAC), conventional landing craft, expeditionary fighting vehicles, and helicopters.

The initial training, and most challenging, was the Senior Officer Ship's Material Readiness Course (SOSMRC), requiring thirteen weeks of training at the Naval Reactors Facility in a sparsely populated area about fifty miles west of Idaho Falls, Idaho. SOSMRC training focuses on operation and management of a ship's steam plant and includes electrical and chemical engineering basics, material readiness, and damage control. Engineering is not a strong suit for me, and frankly, I was a bit concerned about attending this training. SOSMRC brought memories of the Pensacola obstacle course and clearly be another "*Oh Yeah? Watch This!*" challenge. I completed all the courses with decent grades and even scored high on electrical systems and boiler water chemistry, believe it or not.

The next part of our training was at the Surface Warfare School at Newport, Rhode Island. This training included applicable Navy regulations, the "rules of the road" to be followed by ships and other vessels at sea to prevent collision. The training focused on deep draft seamanship and conducting amphibious operations. To train Captains for the decisions at sea, the Navy uses simulators—just as pilots use simulators to train for the sky.

The final step for me was to observe a Landing Platform Dock (LPD) operating at sea. After a few days aboard an LPD operating off the Southern California coast, I flew to the Philippines for further transfer by helicopter to the USS *Vancouver* flight deck. And after a day under way on the *Vancouver*, in an informal change of command at sea, I once again said the words, "I relieve you, sir." I was Captain of the ship.

We operated as part of an Amphibious Ready Group, conducting amphibious training and exercises with embarked Marines in the Western Pacific. My first opportunity to see the *Vancouver*'s capabilities came soon as we operated in the vicinity of Iwo Jima. The *Vancouver* had a well deck with a large ramp that we lowered and then ballasted down and flooded the well deck. This allowed landing craft to move in and out of the flooded zone to carry Marines ashore or return. We also had a flight deck that provided a landing pad for small and large helicopters, enabling them to operate simultaneously with well deck operations. Amphibious operations are impressive but slow-paced compared to carrier flight ops. The slow pace helped my steep learning curve.

One day as we steamed west toward Iwo Jima, I saw that we were getting close to our next turn—but the officer of the deck (OOD) had yet to indicate his intentions. Though we had a large margin of safety, we were heading directly toward the island.

I called to the OOD. "Wouldn't it be special," I said, "to take some sand home to your kids?"

"Sir?"

"You're going to get your chance, so bring some for me." I explained, "Because unless you turn now, in about twenty minutes at this speed, we'll be very close to being on the beach." He got my point.

After a few months of training in the Western Pacific, we returned to our home port, San Diego, for a short stand-down period and time for personal leave. We then conducted additional amphibious training and exercises off the California coast.

Two unplanned events made the next six months anything but routine. First, as we returned to San Diego, we had an engineering casualty. Our engineering plant could not operate until a major portion of the steam system was replaced. We had been scheduled for shipyard overhaul, and San Diego had major shipyard capabilities, but the decision was made to tow us with a tug to San Francisco.

That five-hundred-mile transit took four days. I spent many hours on the bridge looking at the stern of a tugboat moving at the speed of a bicyclist or a long-distance runner. We needed steam to heat the ship and prepare food, so the Navy placed a large portable "donkey boiler" on the flight deck. The challenge was that the boiler had the capacity to heat the ship or prepare food but not both. It was winter, so we did a lot of shivering before mealtime.

When we arrived at Hunter's Point shipyard in the Bay area, the Vancouver was placed in dry dock, and no sooner were we immobile than the shipyard went on strike. There we were, five hundred miles from homeport, with no work scheduled. This was a unique leadership challenge. I maximized training courses and other education opportunities, as well as team sports. I was able to contract with the Cybernetics Leadership Center in San Diego to conduct a professional leadership development course.

And so ended my command tour—with my ship in a dry dock and no work for the officers and crew. However, my highest aspiration was about to be a reality—becoming the Captain of an aircraft carrier.

There were three carriers in San Diego whose Captain billets needed to be filled. I felt confident that would mean I would be able to stay on the West Coast, avoiding a major conflict between career and marriage. Linda's willingness to endure another move was almost zero.

However, the carrier assignments were decided. I would become Captain of the USS *Coral Sea* (CV-43). I had thought that to be unlikely. The *Coral Sea* was the second-oldest carrier in the fleet. The ship was designed to defend against Japanese kamikaze attacks, and she had just completed what was to be her last deployment. The *Coral Sea* needed major repairs and an overhaul, which are expensive investments for an old ship.

Despite those initial reservations, the next twenty months were the best of my Navy career—and after I detached from the *Coral Sea*, the recognition continued. In 1990, I was honored with both the John Paul Jones Award for inspirational leadership from the Navy League of the United States[2] and the Tailhook Association's Tailhooker of the Year Award[3] for excellence in naval aviation leadership.

---

2   The John Paul Jones Award for Inspirational Leadership. John Paul Jones was our Navy's first indomitable sea fighter, whose spirit of personal sacrifice, patriotic devotion, and courage further added to his glory as an inspirational leader. In tribute to one who has followed such a course of honored leadership, the Navy League of the United States makes this award in 1990 to Captain Lloyd Edward Allen Jr., USN, for inspirational leadership in performance of naval service as Commanding Officer, USS *Coral Sea* (CV-43). Captain Allen guided his ship to unparalleled accomplishments during an intensive operating schedule that included the ship's restricted availability, refresher training, advanced, and a Mediterranean Sea deployment during which USS *Coral Sea* performed flawlessly in both the Lebanon hostage crisis and the evacuation of the American Embassy, Beirut. His dedication and astute leadership significantly enhanced the crew's morale and resulted in improvement in all areas of the ship's readiness and material condition. He coordinated operations of the embarked airwing and USS *Coral Sea*, producing a smoothly coordinated, highly effective combat team that proved ready when called upon to show our national resolve. Captain Allen's superb leadership, judgment, and inspiring devotion to duty uphold the highest traditions of the U.S. Naval Service. Presented this on June 4, 1990.

3   1990 Tailhooker of the Year Award, RADM Ed Allen, Commanding Officer, USS *Coral Sea* (CV-43). The Tailhook Association is an independent, fraternal, nonprofit organization, internationally recognized as the premier supporter of the aircraft carrier and other sea-based aviation. The purposes of the association are to foster, encourage, develop, study, and support the aircraft carrier, sea-based aircraft, both fixed and rotary wing, and aircrews of the United States and to educate and inform the public in the appropriate role of the aircraft carrier and carrier aviation in the nation's defense system. The Tailhooker of the Year Award is established as the one individual who, in the judgment of the board of directors, has made the most significant contribution to U.S. carrier aviation.

From the Coral Sea to Midway

As the last Captain of the USS *Coral Sea*, I was fascinated by the carrier's illustrious history—including World War II for which it was named. The Battle of the Coral Sea was the precursor to the Battle of Midway, which halted Japan's expansion in the Pacific and marked a turning point in World War II.

After the surprise attack on Pearl Harbor on December 7, 1941, the Japanese set out with the goal of destroying the U.S. Pacific Fleet and establishing naval supremacy over east Asia and the southwest Pacific.

The attack was only a tactical victory for the Japanese. It was a strategic failure. They did not attack vital onshore facilities, all carriers were at sea that morning, and the Navy leadership was unharmed. Meanwhile, the attack unified the American people and brought the United States into the war.

Japan proceeded to occupy Burma, Malaysia, Singapore, Indonesia, and the Philippines, ensuring access to natural resources, including oil and rubber. The Japanese then decided to invade and occupy Port Moresby in New Guinea and Tulagi in the Solomon Islands to protect their right flank in Indonesia and take away a strong base for Allied attacks.

After the United States deciphered Japanese naval messages, Admiral Nimitz ordered all four Pacific Fleet carriers to the Coral Sea, off the northeast coast of Australia, where Japan's task force included two carriers and a light cruiser. That set the stage for the Battle of the Coral Sea, which would make victory at Midway possible.

Coral Sea was the first pure carrier-versus-carrier battle in history, as neither surface fleet had sighted the other. In the battle, both sides suffered severe damages to their carriers, including the USS

Lexington and the Japanese carrier *Shōkaku*. The Coral Sea battle left the Japanese without enough planes to cover the ground attack of Port Moresby, resulting in a strategic Allied victory. The Allies had stopped the Japanese advance for the first time.

The Battle of Midway came four weeks later, from June 4 to 7, 1942, six months after Pearl Harbor. The Japanese strategy was to lure American aircraft carriers into a trap and occupy Midway to extend Japan's defensive perimeter. However, American cryptographers broke enough code to determine the date and location of the planned attack and enabled an ambush.

Japan lost four carriers, a cruiser, and 292 aircraft and suffered 2,500 casualties. The United States lost the Yorktown, the destroyer USS *Hammann*, and 145 aircraft and suffered 307 casualties.

The loss of the four carriers put Japan on the defensive, stopping its expansion in the Pacific and destroying its capacity to invade Australia. The Battle of Midway went down in history as a decisive victory for the U.S. Navy and a major turning point of the war in the Pacific Theater. The Battle of the Coral Sea was an essential part of Midway being possible.

CHAPTER 9

"THE AGELESS WARRIOR"

Command of the USS *Coral Sea* (CV-43) was the second and most significant of my "mountaintop" experiences. I was where I was supposed to be and doing what I was supposed to be doing. This was my "magnificent obsession."

Once again, with the words "I relieve you, sir," I assumed a new command. It was June 12, 1988. The tugs had maneuvered the *USS Coral Sea* away from Pier 12 at Naval Station Norfolk into the Elizabeth River. I had "the conn," meaning I was solely responsible for orders to the helmsman and lee helmsman for the ship's speed and heading. The traffic and weather were ideal, with light winds and two- to three-foot seas—"ceiling and visibility unlimited."

Standing on the bridge of the *USS Coral Sea* underway for the first time, I looked out on the Thimble Shoals Channel. I glanced left at the Captain's chair. In all my many hours of standing bridge watches on other carriers, I was always confident knowing that whatever happened, the experienced presence, wisdom, and decision-making would always be in that chair. Now that chair was empty. It was my chair now. I was *the* Commanding Officer of "the Ageless Warrior," guiding her out the Chesapeake and onward to the Atlantic.

It Starts and Ends at the Top

In 1988, the USS *Coral Sea* (CV-43) was scheduled to be decommissioned after one last deployment. I had become her final Captain. In twenty months, the carrier's readiness would rise from near the bottom to near the top.

How did it happen?

In short, I inherited a crew filled with pride and commitment. In these first few weeks, I earned their trust. My mantra to the ship's officers was that "if you wear khaki, your job is to take care of the sailors"—to train them for their mission and promote their health and welfare.

That commitment starts and ends at the top.

Here is how Joseph Conrad put it in *Command at Sea: The Prestige, Privilege and Burden of Command*:

> *Only a seaman realizes to what great extent an entire ship reflects the personality and ability of one individual, her Commanding Officer. To a landsman, this is not understandable—and sometimes it is even difficult for us to comprehend—but it is so! A ship at sea is a different world in herself, and in consideration of the protracted and distant operations of the fleet units, the Navy must place great power, responsibility and trust in the hands of those leaders chosen for command. In each ship there is one man who, in the hour of emergency or peril at sea, can turn to no other man. There is one who alone is ultimately responsible for the safe navigation, engineering performance, accurate gunfire and morale of the ship. He is the*

> *Commanding Officer. He is the ship. This is the most difficult and demanding assignment in the Navy. There is not an instant during his tour as Commanding Officer that he can escape the grasp of command responsibility. His privileges, in view of his obligations, are almost ludicrously small; nevertheless, this is the spur which has given the Navy its great leaders. It is a duty which richly deserves the highest, time-honored title of the seafaring world—Captain.*

As we transited the channel, I looked down on the four-acre flight deck and considered the power and potential of the ship and the Air Wing team. I mused about the major carrier operations that we would be conducting, day and night, in all weather and all sea states, with little margin for error. Every step was critical, whether in flight or when entering or leaving port. Each move mattered when replenishing fuel and supplies at sea or when maneuvering in restricted or high-traffic waters. One failure in the chain of events could mean disaster.

We had to be ready for the unexpected, and that meant working as an experienced and a competent team. A man overboard, a cascade of electrical failures, a collision, flooding, or fire on the flight deck during launch and recovery, all possible. I mentally rehearsed all those contingencies and more, and I put the bridge teams through informal training sessions.

I knew that I would need to manage my physical and mental energies if I expected to conduct daily operations and still be able to handle emergencies. I conditioned myself to sleep, or at least rest, during the short periods between flight launches and recoveries. A twenty-hour day was normal, and by taking short daytime naps, I made it possible.

Our eventual deployment with the Sixth Fleet would take us to the Mediterranean. I visualized the countries along that seashore, the

OH YEAH? WATCH THIS!

situations we could face, and the possibilities for offensive strike and air superiority missions.

Those missions would be executed by the Air Wing Aircraft: F/A-18 Strike Fighters, A-6E Bombers, EA-6Bs for Electronic Warfare, E-2 Hawkeye for airborne surveillance and early warning, S-3A Viking for antisubmarine warfare, and SH-3 rotary wing for sea combat and sea strike.

I constantly asked myself the question: "What needs to be done that only the Captain can do?" I tried to make the most of what I could do. Every day, over the ship's announcing system, I spoke about immediate and upcoming operations and events. I reviewed what was going well and not so well. I recognized individuals for special performance. I offered accurate information to dispel any rumors and falsehoods. We held frequent awards ceremonies, and every few weeks I recorded an audiotape that was mailed to Norfolk for crew members' families and friends to access. In those days before the rise of the internet, that was a way to let them hear directly from the Captain.

Each week, a different work center would muster on the hangar deck for a morning inspection. I began with a personnel inspection, which gave me at least a short face-to-face interaction with each sailor. I defined what was expected and how it should be executed, restated our schedule, and reviewed whatever needed closer attention. I would frequently call a sailor front and center for unexpected recognition. I would say, Petty Officer Jones is what a *Coral Sea* sailor looks like. I would give him special liberty for a day.

I understood that food service and quality were essential to morale. At times, particularly on holidays, I would serve meals myself. I can tell you that a sleepy sailor, up early and standing in line for half an hour, will feel wide awake when he sees his Captain serving him scrambled eggs and bacon.

The sailors could see that their Captain put a high priority on their quality of life. Sometimes when I learned of a sailor with a pressing family situation, I personally would relieve him for a holiday so that he could be with loved ones. "I've got this watch," I would say. "You go celebrate Christmas, and we'll see you in the morning."

Another essential was the quality of the crew's "berthing" area or living quarters. Each sailor had only a bed, a.k.a. "rack," and kept all personal belongings in a cramped storage space under the frame. Above the rack was a small fluorescent light by which he could read a magazine or write a letter at day's end—not easy if the light doesn't work. At one point, I had a fellow officer guarantee me that all lights would be repaired before he finished duty that day.

Once, when I noticed that the single TV in the berthing area wasn't working, I asked a Chief Petty Officer (CPO) to turn it on. "It doesn't work," he said. "We have one on order." I said that I believed there was a fine TV in the CPO's mess that seemed to be working well. Somehow, he discovered another one that was not being used and had it installed. Small things matter, perhaps, but very big ones for the crew's morale.

The Greatest Show on Earth

Looking down at the flight deck from the Captain's chair on the bridge, I could see officers, CPOs, and sailors wearing flight deck jerseys in a variety of colors, each identifying a specific area of responsibility.[4] Flight deck crews are organized into specialized teams that execute their responsibilities with seamless precision. In that way, they are like a symphony, delivering a production of large scale through the discipline of individual sections fulfilling their functions.

A symphony produces beautiful music in a clean, healthy, climate-controlled environment. The audience is generally of mature age and exhibits cultivated manners while focusing on one harmonious performance. Everyone is in a relaxed, pleasant mood, enjoying the moment. If someone misses a key, there's always the next show to get it just right. That's where the comparison ends.

The flight deck crew, by contrast, labors amid the deafening roar of jet engines in temperatures ranging from subfreezing cold to searing desert heat. Everything is in motion, sailors, aircraft, equipment, most of the aircraft costing many tens of millions of dollars and each life precious. Most of the crew members are eighteen to twenty-one years

---

4   The colors of the flight deck:
   - *Yellow:* aircraft handling officer, catapult and arresting gear officer and plane directors.
   - *Green:* catapult and arresting gear crew and Air Wing maintenance personnel.
   - *Red:* firefighters and damage control party; crash and salvage crew; explosive ordnance disposal.
   - *Purple:* aviation fuel handlers.
   - *Blue:* trainee plane handler; chocks, chains, and aircraft moves; elevator operators and tractor drivers.
   - *Brown:* squadron plane Captains prepare aircraft for flight, manage movement, and monitor servicing.
   - *Black/white checkered:* landing signal officer; aircraft final checker; squadron plane inspector/troubleshooter; air transfer officer; liquid oxygen crew; safety and medical personnel.

old. Their typical day is twelve to eighteen hours. They launch and recover aircraft in cycles of about one and a half hours, sleeping in cramped quarters. Failure to execute each step correctly could cause minor or major injuries

During pre-launch, all airplanes are inspected, required maintenance performed, inspections completed, full fuel confirmed, and ordinance loaded (but not armed until in a safe area). The flight deck systems are activated including preparation for fires, major or minor mishaps, and ability to render medical aid and assistance. The flight crews proceed to their assigned planes and complete final inspections.

Then each plane taxies forward to be spotted on the catapult. Once in position, the catapult shuttle locks on to its nose gear—and with all systems checked, the catapult fires.

Now imagine an eighteen-wheeler, filled with cargo, parked on the highway. That's about the weight of a fully loaded F-14 Tomcat. What sort of unfathomable force would it take to get that rig barreling down the road at 170 miles an hour within two seconds and two hundred feet? What would that scene look like?

Keep in mind, we are talking about multi-million-dollar aircraft being catapulted every minute or so with lives depending on success with each launch.

That's the job an aircraft catapult must accomplish. In the daytime, the spectacle is exhilarating. At nighttime, it can be terrifying. At any time, it's a miracle. It is Act 1 of the greatest show on Earth.

When missions are complete, Act 2 begins when all aircraft return to the carrier. They rendezvous and fly an established carrier approach. The approach altitude is 800 feet at three miles. The aircraft fly over the right side of the ship and "break" 180 degrees into the landing pattern, establishing fifty- to sixty-second intervals between aircraft.

On the downwind turn, the pilot descends to 600 feet. Landing gear, flaps, and slats are extended. The tailhook has already been extended and checked by the wingman. When abeam the landing area, the pilot turns and slowly descends to about 450 feet at 90 degrees, crossing the ship's wake and lining up with the flight deck.

At that point, the carrier is three-quarters of a mile ahead. The pilot can see the landing area and the white centerline on the angled deck. On the carrier, a Landing Signal Officer (LSO), who is an experienced carrier pilot, establishes visual contact and provides advisory calls on the airspeed, the lineup, and the angle of attack. The officer uses the signal lights of an Optical Landing System to guide the pilot in adjusting the glide slope—too high, too low, or right on.

Meanwhile, the bridge team is focusing on the wind velocity and the carrier speed and heading, all of which play crucial roles. The combination of wind and ship speed should equal thirty knots. Lower than that, and the flight ops become more difficult.

The pilot now is "in the groove," and the plane will touch down in eighteen to twenty seconds. To fly precisely, the pilot must make continuous minor adjustments. The tailhook must hit the deck in the area of four arresting cables, which are spaced at fifty-foot intervals. The pilot's goal is to snag the No. 3 wire with the tailhook, at the center of the landing area.

The aircraft is approaching at 130–150 knots when it touches down on the angled deck, which is only 550 feet long. When the tailhook engages the arresting cable, the aircraft stops within about 400 feet. This happens in about two seconds. In a couple of heartbeats, the cable decelerates an aircraft to a dead stop.

Within a minute the next flight will be coming in, so the hook must be immediately retracted and wings folded to allow the plane to taxi forward to park in the bow area. A crew comes out to refuel and rearm each plane and provide needed maintenance. Soon enough it will be time for the next launch.

The Captain's Mast: Justice at Sea

I looked into the eyes of the sailor standing before me. "What would your mother say," I asked him, "if she knew that you just pleaded guilty of what you were accused of here today?" I was conducting a Captain's Mast, part of the Uniform Code of Military Justice, UCMJ authorizing a ship's Captain to mete out justice for minor offenses. I served as the prosecution, defense, and judge.

"I don't think she'd like it too much," the sailor responded. He was standing before me in dress uniform, accompanied by officers in charge.

"Well, then, let's give her a call and find out," I said. We were in port, and I had arranged in advance for her to be waiting for a phone call during the proceeding. I knew this young man had strong family ties. My practice was to review the defendant's record, looking for information that would trigger a gut response—some fact about his family, his hometown, or something that appealed to his pride.

"Here she is," I said, handing him the phone. "She wants you to tell her all about it." Puzzled, he spoke into the receiver. "Uh, Mom?" And we listened as he tried to explain to her what was going on. I knew that his mother's words would be far more effective than anything I could say.

"Case dismissed," I said after he hung up, looking deeply contrite. "But never forget: your mother deserves better behavior from her son." I don't recall his offense. That's not the point. What I do know is that this was a day that he would remember for a lifetime.

At a Captain's Mast, I had the authority to discipline and impose punishment for minor offenses without a trial. If I found a man guilty, the punishment could include a reprimand, restriction to the ship, extra duty, a reduction in rank, or half pay for up to two months.

I conducted the proceedings standing at a podium. The defendant would enter a plea and then had an opportunity to state his case and discuss it with those present.

On one occasion, I had noted that the accused hailed from Fredericksburg, in my home state of Texas. I was familiar with this small town in the Hill Country of Texas. It was the home of Chester W. Nimitz, the Five-star Fleet Admiral who commanded Pacific naval operations in World War II—and became the namesake of the USS *Nimitz* supercarrier.

"So tell me," I asked the defendant, "what would the good people of Fredericksburg think if I asked you to run through the streets of town with a yellow stripe painted down your back?" He paled noticeably. I continued, "You do know that's the same hometown as the great Chester Nimitz, don't you?"

He paused and then respectfully replied, "Isn't he the mechanic on plane 104?" Among those attending, I heard gasps and some outright laughter. Case dismissed.

While I was Commanding Officer of the USS *Vancouver* LPD-2, another young man was accused of a more serious offense while we were in port. He had a girlfriend in Tijuana and had been returning a few hours or a day late from these visits—but this time, he had just disappeared. We were preparing a desertion report for being AWOL (Absent Without Leave), when the phone rang in my office.

"I was abducted by gang members in San Diego," he told me. "But Captain, I've escaped now! Don't pay the ransom!" Creative, yes. And guilty, too. We picked him up and gave him a ride back to the ship, where he was confined for sixty days.

Several years ago, I received an email from a former USS *Vancouver* sailor. He wrote, "Captain, I don't know if you remember me, but I was a Petty Officer Second Class aboard the Vancouver when you were the Captain."

I did indeed remember him. He was responsible for managing the ship's supplies. He had an alcohol problem. I found him guilty, reduced him in rank, cut his pay for a month, and required either thirty days of restrictions or attendance at Alcoholics Anonymous meetings for thirty consecutive days. He chose the latter, first in San Diego and then at meetings aboard ship at sea.

"Captain, I want you to know that since the time I stood before you at Mast, I haven't had a drink," he wrote. He had dedicated his life to helping others seeking sobriety and later became a Navy Drug/Rehab Counselor. "I'll never forget your words, Captain. You looked me in the eye and said, 'You have not done your duty, and others have had to take up the slack. I needed you, and you've disappointed me.'"

This gentleman wanted me to know, after all these years, that what had touched him, what had motivated him to change and to pursue a career helping others, was the knowledge that someone had valued him. Someone had been counting on him. If I had valued him enough to be disappointed, that meant I had seen something worthwhile in him, and he was determined to become the man he knew he could be.

Just Another Day at the "Office"

"Captain, this might not work out," the officer of the deck whispered to me. I responded in my confident command voice: "We've prepared for challenges like this. It's training that money can't buy. Just do your duty. Stay focused." What I was thinking, though, was a bit different:

What if the kid is right and it doesn't work out? I might wind up back on the farm.

The Ageless Warrior was returning to her home port of Norfolk, Virginia, after three weeks of intensive training. The last thirteen miles, from abeam the Fort Story lighthouse at the entrance to Chesapeake Bay to our berth at the Norfolk Naval Base, was through the Thimble Shoals channel. It is a narrow passage with no way to turn around.

The *Coral Sea* crew was particularly eager to return home that Friday evening. We were scheduled to get under way the next morning for the Dependents Day Cruise for several hundred family members. We would be heading back out the channel to the Atlantic, where we would operate the ship for several hours before returning late afternoon. This was a rare opportunity for the families to observe carrier operations. The highlight would be an air power demonstration by the Air Wing. The guests would see flight operations, catapult launches, and arrested landings and then watch an air show demonstrating tactical power at sea.

This event was a big deal. But as always, I was thinking first about safety and security of the ship and crew. We headed toward the channel with both wind and visibility at the edge of what would be considered safe transit. Should we proceed? I weighed the factors—one of which was the opportunity to give the crew some great training. It would build confidence in themselves, and it would help me confirm my own confidence in the bridge team.

I postponed my decision for half an hour and then did a final review of all the risk factors. I felt confident. "Officer of the Deck," I called out, "let's do it." We headed into the channel, and at that point, there was no turning back. We were committed. It *had* to work out.

At three miles in, the wind decreased, but so did the visibility. I could barely see the bow. Navigating by high-resolution radar, I stayed laser-focused on the reflective buoys marking the channel. I had rehearsed such scenarios in my mind many times. This navigation required my steadfast attention, but I knew I could do it safely. After all, I had the channel to myself—until I *didn't*! It's always what you think you know but don't; that will be your undoing.

"Coral Sea, you have an outbound tanker," the radio informed me. It was Norfolk traffic control. I immediately radioed the tanker's Captain, and we confirmed our position and intentions. Years before GPS, I continued to navigate by radar. The other Captain and I stayed in continuous communication. Finally, I saw the tanker's bow, and we passed port to port and well clear.

As we steamed into port, the wind picked up. Not a major concern—not yet, anyway. We reduced speed to bare steerage, and eight tugs came out to maneuver us pier-side. As we began backing into the pier, the wind velocity increased quickly, and we were at risk of our stern taking out the end of the pier.

"All ahead full!" the harbor pilot ordered the tugs.

The First Lieutenant, stationed on the stern, could see what was coming. He radioed me: "Captain, this is going to be close." Soon after came the words I was waiting for: "All clear, Captain. That was close. *Very* close!" By ten o'clock at night, we had secured the ship at the pier, and we could try to relax and get some sleep. *All in all, just another day at the office!*

At 5:30 the next morning, we embarked several hundred family members for the Dependents Day Cruise. We headed out from the pier—the one that the ship almost took out the night before—and back through the thirteen-mile channel to the Atlantic. The weather off the Virginia coast was beautiful, with clear blue skies and light winds—perfect for the day's activities.

The Air Wing demonstrations began with the catapult launches, or "cat-shots." Each type of aircraft simulated its mission. Air-to-air missiles were fired at simulated targets as well as bombing smoke targets. The E-2C Airborne Early Warning and the EA6-B Electronic Warfare did a flyby as the narrator explained the surveillance function and ability to detect and jam enemy radar. The SH-3 demonstrated their Sea Control capabilities and performed an actual search and rescue of a man overboard. "The man" was a dummy named Oscar.

After about forty-five minutes, the flight deck was cleared and the Air Wing, recovered. The *Coral Sea* returned to Norfolk through the Thimble Shoals channel. It was a demonstration of air power with awe-inspiring sights and thunderous sounds that I am confident the Navy families will remember for a lifetime.

Faithfully at My Side

During my service as Captain, Marine Corporal Lance Parris Ponton was assigned as my orderly to ensure my safety and security. Wherever I went he accompanied me, striving to be inconspicuous—which is no small feat for a 6-foot-1, 185-pound marine with 8 percent body fat. Donna asked him to share some memories from that time, and here is what he wrote:

> *I was at Captain Allen's side wherever he went on the ship. Most of the time he was on the bridge or in his state room, but he spent much time with the sailors.*
>
> *When off the ship, I would drive the Captain to his destinations. On one such occasion I drove him to an event in Norfolk, Va. On the way back, he was sitting in the back reading a newspaper that blocked my view from the mirror. A car drove out in front of me*

at an intersection and we crashed into its side. Captain Allen flew over the front seat and landed head first in the passenger seat. I just knew I was about to be in a lot of trouble! But he just picked himself up, made sure I was all right, and after we got back to the base, he told me to go get another Navy car. He never complained or griped to me about the accident.

There were no "typical days." Sometimes he would jog on the flight deck, and I would go with him when he suggested it. In the morning, I always tried to be at the door of the Captain's Cabin before he left. He would tell me what was on the agenda for the day, and I'd take care of any request he had. If he had none, I would just stand on the bridge while he was in his raised seat looking out over the flight deck.

I was the escort for Barbara Mandrell after she flew out to the ship. The Captain assigned me to escort her around the ship for the few days she was going to be on board. On the last day of her visit, the Coral Sea pulled back into Norfolk. That evening the Captain hosted the Barbara Mandrell show in the hangar bay, and a lot of high-ranking officers and officials came to the show. I was surprised when Captain Allen, sitting on the front row with his family and lots of brass around him, told me to take a seat next to him on the front row. I never imagined I would have been so honored!

And then Barbara Mandrell, on stage in front of at least two thousand people, said she wanted to say a special thanks to someone who had blessed her with a great stay on the Coral Sea. I just knew she was about to thank Captain Allen. Nope! She thanked Lance Corporal Ponton—and then walked down off the stage and kissed me in front of all those folks.

Captain Allen made a tremendous impression on my life. He taught me the value of an education. I was blown away by all his achievements and his continued pursuit of higher education. He educated and trained his officers as if their life depended on it—and often it did. He put together training programs and opportunities for his officers and brought in guest speakers. Captain Allen demonstrated the benefits of higher education and made it real to me.

As Captain, he was revered by everyone, yet he was truly a humble man. You could tell that he loved his crewmen. He was very approachable and treated everyone with respect. He showed great character to me.

Captain Allen had an exemplary work ethic, with a commitment to excellence in everything he did. Even as a young Marine, I couldn't keep up with the Old Man! He took care of his ship, his crew, and his officers. He worked hard and expected the best from everyone who worked for him. Most of those who worked under him recognized that drive in him, and that motivated them to be their best, too.

Captain Allen made it a point to recognize and congratulate people for their achievements. Sometimes it was just a smile and a handshake or an "attaboy," but he was quick to encourage others.

Captain Allen practiced leadership through example. He was determined not just to do well, but to be the best. He was smart, always up-to-date on everything, and never wavered in the face of uncertainty or pressure. It was an honor to serve him—and an even greater honor just to know him.

★ ★

CHAPTER 10

FROM THE BEST OF TIMES TO THE WORST OF TIMES

I had every reason to feel confident in a bright future as I departed the USS *Coral Sea*. For eighteen years, my career encompassed four previous commands and led the *Coral Sea* on her last deployment, finishing with extraordinary readiness and performance. I received the Legion of Merit and two other prestigious awards. Yet despite all of this, I had a sense of foreboding and guilt about a failing marriage. There was no joy or sense of celebration. Perhaps this was part of the reason I took on a sense of pride and exaggerated sense of self-importance.

After the Rear Admiral selections were announced in 1990, I enjoyed a stream of calls and cards and letters. Naval officers, from ensign to Four Star Admiral, offered their congratulations. So did relatives, classmates, and friends.

Then came the Flag Officer indoctrination at the Pentagon, a week of briefings and dinners and receptions, including one in the National Naval Museum at the historic Washington Navy Yard. Linda was available to join me for a few of those occasions.

"Before your head gets too big," the Vice Chief of Naval Operations said during one of the briefings, "I remind you that there were at least five other flag-eligible Captains whose records of performance were just as good as yours." Your selection was not a reward for performance, he said, but rather an assessment of leadership potential.

My first flag assignment was Commander at the Naval Space Command in Dahlgren, Virginia, eighty miles southeast of the Pentagon. Naval Space Command was a small, focused group of military and civilian experts in the use of reconnaissance and communications satellites.

Much of my weekdays were filled with briefings and with traveling to briefings. I reported to the Chief of Naval Operations at the Pentagon on programming and budgeting issues and the Four Star Air Force General in Colorado Springs who commanded all U.S. Space Forces. I had no direct experience in the field. Until then, I had been an end user of space-age capabilities. It was my responsibility to become knowledgeable as quickly as possible and to be effective in this role.

Collision Course

Once again, my Navy career and my marriage were on a collision course. I would need to relocate to Dahlgren. Would Linda and Ashley, who was now in high school, be coming with me? Or would they stay in Virginia Beach? If they came with me, Linda would be setting aside her professional work at Norfolk State University, and Ashley would have to transfer from her high school.

Dahlgren was not Virginia Beach. It was a more rural area, with a different culture and social life. Linda and I visited Dahlgren to check it out, and she had little appetite for what she saw. As for me, I had little appetite for revisiting the stress of our previous relocations. I didn't have it in me to go through that again.

I decided that living alone would be the less troubling option for all of us, so I moved into the Bachelor Officers Quarters at Dahlgren. I told myself that I could commute home on weekends, three and a half hours each way, and that we could make it work. What I was doing was avoiding the truth that my Navy career and our family life were continuing on a collision course.

During my time in Dahlgren, I had little in the way of a social life. The nearest movie theater was in Fredericksburg about thirty miles west. I spent my weekday evenings in Dahlgren reading, planning, and focusing on fitness. Had I lived with my family in the flag quarters, I could have done a better job representing the Navy in the community. Instead, I was a party of one, living in a remote location, devoting my energies to a field in which I lacked experience. I was not giving the Navy or family their just due. It was not my finest hour.

Assignment: Joint Chiefs of Staff, the Pentagon

My Naval Space Command tour ended sooner than I expected when I got orders in October 1991 to report to the Joint Chiefs of Staff at the Pentagon as Deputy Director for Current Operations. The Joint Staff, made up of officers from all the military services, has eight directorates. I was assigned to J-3 Operations, which coordinates operational plans.

It was a job that took me to the highest levels of responsibility, interacting with the chairman and the staffs of combatant Commanders. I was included in the planning of any ongoing or current military operations.

My daily schedule was filled with meetings, preparing contingency strikes, and coordinating with my counterparts on the Combatant Commanders' staffs. Other areas of responsibility included humanitarian support, Special Operations Forces, and the Special Technical Operations Division, and I represented the Joint Staff on the military's role on the War on Drugs. Most of the current operations issues involved enforcement of no-fly zones in Iraq and humanitarian and disaster relief. We provided assistance in Bosnia and Herzegovina and to famine-stricken Somalia, as well as disaster relief within the United States, notably in the aftermath of Hurricane Andrew.

This time, I could avoid the hassle of a weekday commute. I found an apartment that I shared with another naval officer within walking distance of the Pentagon and next to the Pentagon City Mall with easy access to restaurants, theaters, and shopping.

My weekends were unpredictable. I expected that I would be going back to Virginia Beach often but quickly found myself staying in town if there were any significant military operations or developments. I wouldn't know until late Friday if going home would be possible—and it felt next to impossible even when I could go. It was a 200-mile trip each way, with heavy traffic on I-95 and I-64 and often during foul weather. And so I found myself staying in Washington on many weekends. I spent the time socializing with friends and going to sports events, movies, and concerts.

It took only a few of those weekends to conclude that it wasn't going to work out as I had hoped—and not just the commute but my personal life too. I was returning Sunday to start a long week at the Pentagon feeling drained, not refreshed. I had reached my limit.

"I Can't Do This Anymore"

One Sunday afternoon as I was driving back to Washington and about to enter the Hampton Bay Bridge Tunnel, I looked across the bay and the Elizabeth River. The sunset was magnificent, with streaks of orange through cirrus clouds. I had a sense of serenity. That image, in vivid detail, stayed with me through the tunnel as I emerged into twilight.

Somewhere around Williamsburg, the darkness settled in. I saw another flash of orange, this time from the dashboard of my Datsun 280ZX. The sunset light dimmed, and so did my serenity. I felt confusion, angst, resignation. Then I heard my own voice, shouting, "I can't do this anymore!"

I didn't know what, but something had to change! I think of that as my Garden of Gethsemane moment. I prayed that God could spare me the anguish. I had been keeping a tight fist of control over my life and *"Oh Watch This"* did not apply. Now I felt that grip begin to let go. I recalled Isaiah 4:10: "Do not be dismayed, for I am your God. I will strengthen you and help you. I will uphold you."

My marriage was a mess. For years I had made the Navy my career to the point of not taking decisive action to lead my family back on course. My ambitions had blinded me to the reality of our relationship. I liked to think I was good at fixing things but not this. I didn't know what to do, so I tried not to think about it. I was a military leader in the world's premier power, and here I was telling God that I didn't know what to do about my personal life.

I thought again of that time many years earlier when I waved farewell to Linda from the flight deck of the USS *Enterprise*. It was full steam ahead for the ship and for my career—and yet Linda, lost in the crowd on the pier, looked sad and abandoned. I had proved since that I could command an aircraft carrier, but I couldn't fix a marriage.

I had been starting to doubt myself, and at times I felt angry and resentful. I recalled seeing an old oak tree, years earlier, that had been felled by a hurricane. Once stately, it now lay on the ground, its huge roots exposed and dangling in the sunlight. My marriage was like that. I could see how and why it had suffered, but how could I replant what was so badly ripped? I simply lacked the physical and emotional energy to reconcile family and career, and I saw no answer to that dilemma.

Not that we didn't keep trying. For several months I spent as many weekends in Virginia Beach that Joint Staff commitments would allow. Linda and I tried individual and couples counseling. I went to several churches and Al-Anon meetings looking for some path of resolution. I found no answers. I filed for divorce.

Separation and divorce are private matters, and I'm uncomfortable addressing that part of my life. The purpose of this book, however, is to tell my story, and that includes how I handled this very difficult experience and what I learned from it.

Command of Carrier Battle Strike Group

I finished my tour with the Joint Staff at the Pentagon in February 1993. I was awarded the Defense Superior Service Medal for my performance as Deputy Director of Current Operations and contributions to national security. Once again I was cited for leadership, planning and attention to detail.

Another significant event occurred when my old college roommate visited me in Washington one weekend. He was the founding partner of a Texas-based law firm, and we would get together from time to time when he came to the firm's District of Columbia office.

"We're having a reception tonight at the office," he said. "Why don't you join us? We'd enjoy your company, and I'm sure you'll like the dinner." As it turned out, there was more to like that evening than the food. He introduced me to his Business Operations Manager, Donna Cook, who lived in Dallas. I sat next to her at dinner. She was attractive and professional, and I felt at ease in conversation with her.

Here's someone I hope I can get to know better, I thought as we talked. And I did. After Donna returned to Dallas, we stayed in touch. We talked for hours and later visited each other. She became my confidant, and over time our relationship deepened. Slowly and surely she was giving me her heart, and that was the gift of a lifetime.

After my Joint Staff assignment, I was selected to command a Carrier Battle Strike Group. This was an opportunity to return to leadership at sea, where I was at my best—and professionally, this assignment clearly would be the best one for me. Still, I was reluctant to execute those orders. I seriously considered requesting an assignment ashore of lesser importance.

This was a career-defining decision. I had worked hard for success in the Navy. The Navy had continued to invest in me, entrusting me with increasing responsibilities, and would rightfully expect my continued service. I thought that to turn this assignment down would signal a lack of loyalty to the Navy and to my shipmates, and yet I knew that my energy and motivation were being depleted.

I would be reporting to Vice Admiral Tony Less, a man of extraordinary wisdom and talent for whom I had worked twice in the past. I explained my reluctance to accept the Strike Group orders. He listened carefully to my dilemma and expressed confidence and support. He gave me a wide berth to make my decision. I took a few days to weigh the pros and cons. After some long and prayerful walks, and with some uncertainty and reluctance, I decided to assume the duties as Commander Carrier Group 4.

Ready to Fight and Win

A *Carrier Battle Group* (CVBG) is a group of warfighting ships centered around a nuclear-powered aircraft carrier with seventy fighter, attack, antisubmarine, and electronic warfare aircraft. The other ships are Aegis Guided-Missile Cruisers (CG), Guided Missile Destroyers (DDG), and Logistic Support Ships and Oiler (AOE/AOR). The CVBG deploys and fights as a single unit to conduct surface, air, and subsurface warfare. It operates day and night in all kinds of weather.

Before deployment, the ships and aircraft focus on unit training independently and then come together to train as one group. The CCG-4 staff was a group of seasoned military professionals and experts in air, surface, and subsurface warfare. They had the experience and competency to evaluate the leadership and combat readiness of the officers and crew in their respective missions of the ships and aircraft.

That readiness was accomplished through integrated training and real-world exercises. The decision as to my Battle Group's combat readiness was based on observed performance, its scores on exercises, and my staff's professional assessment. The final decision was mine alone, based on the answer to a simple question: *Is this Battle Group ready on arrival to fight and win?*

During the next few months, we deployed with five different Battle Groups for final training: the *America, Saratoga, George Washington, Roosevelt*, and *Dwight D. Eisenhower*. We used threat-based exercises that stressed the limits of warfighting readiness. I then certified the Battle Group as combat ready to go into harm's way. Certification is not guaranteed. In one case, my assessment was that the Battle Group was not fully combat ready, and it conducted additional training en route to its assigned overseas area.

Most of my time during the deployment I was on the carrier, but I spent a day on each of the other ships and flew with the squadrons in the Air Wing. I met with the Commanding Officer, Executive Officer, and Command Master Chief on each ship and was briefed on the ship's readiness. Then I toured all the ship's major spaces, engineering, operations, and so forth, and I ate with the crew on the mess decks.

My tour of duty was complete. The Change of Command was held on the carrier at sea, and I was awarded the Legion of Merit.

Two years before my retirement, I violated two Navy Regulations. An investigation substantiated part of the allegations, and I did not disagree with the findings. I accepted full responsibility for the consequences of my actions.

A New Life

What next? I was informed that I had been "penciled in" for an assignment with an even higher level of responsibility—a level at which success would carry a high probability of promotion to a third star. I made a tough decision: I requested a less-demanding assignment ashore, preferably on the East Coast. Ashley was starting college at Radford University in Virginia, and I felt I needed to be closer to her and to manage some personal matters. In a sense, I moved over to a slower lane and knew that I would be retiring after this final tour. I was at peace with this decision.

The Navy honored my request. I was assigned to the Navy Space and Warfare Command, later renamed the Naval Information Warfare Systems Command. It was responsible for acquisition and evaluation of technology-based systems and networks.

Meanwhile, Donna and I committed to marriage. We were planning a fall wedding, but then I was assigned Temporary Duty to Saudi Arabia as the deputy Commander for air operations. We decided to marry before I left, and in three weeks Donna planned our wedding and prepared the food for the rehearsal dinner and wedding for two hundred guests. Immediately afterward I was off to the Middle East. Donna remained in Dallas to transition out of the law firm. She joined me in Europe after I completed my assignment, and we toured Venice and Vincenza in Italy, Garmisch in Germany, and Oberammergau in Austria.

When we returned to the States, I was assigned quarters in the Washington Navy Yard. I moved from Norfolk, Donna moved from Dallas, and we started our life together, positive and confident about our future. I felt proud to be living in "the Yard" on Admiral's Row, a nineteenth-century section of living quarters for senior officers. We were assigned Quarters V, which had been a medical facility during the Civil War.

My commute was now just five miles to the Command Headquarters in the Crystal City section of Arlington, Virginia. I was assigned leadership and management duties in support of the Commander of SPAWAR. Donna got a position that had predictable hours with a District of Columbia law firm. At first the firm was skeptical how her soft-spoken southern demeanor would fit in with the K-Street culture, but she soon proved her mettle.

Initially it was just the two of us, along with Donna's two dogs, Judge and Lady. Ashley came to live with us in June and attended college locally. The next year Ashley began working part-time with Donna at the law firm. Donna's son, Michael, had completed Navy boot camp in San Diego and was stationed in Norfolk with an E-2C

Hawkeye squadron. He deployed on the USS *America* as part of the flight deck crew doing troubleshooting for squadron aircraft.

Notwithstanding the challenges that come with a second marriage, we faced the future with gratitude and confidence. We felt an easing of the stress in our lives. We were included in events and ceremonies with senior military and civilian leaders. Our neighbors at the Navy Yard organized a surprise shivaree for us when we moved in, and our first guest was Admiral Mike Boorda, Chief of Naval Operations. We enjoyed entertaining small social gatherings of friends.

Donna quickly adapted to being the wife of an Admiral, and the other Navy and Marine Corps wives warmly accepted her. She showed her gracious hospitality and warmth. One day she stopped at the Navy Yard entrance and asked the Marine guards their names. They responded crisply with a salute, giving their ranks and full identities. Donna smiled. "Now that's just fine," she said, "but what does your mother call you?"

Because many of the Marines had nothing special to do for the holidays, Donna invited them to join our family for Thanksgiving dinner. We had two sittings to accommodate them, and the formality quickly vanished. Such was life with Donna during that first year of our marriage as we established the patterns that would see us through many years to come.

Two Telephone Calls

Donna and I soon received two life-changing telephone calls. The Bethesda Naval Hospital Breast Cancer Center called Donna with a diagnosis of an early stage of breast cancer. It had not metastasized. We discussed our options.

"Let's do whatever gives me the greatest chance of spending time with my future grandchildren," Donna told me as we weighed the options. She underwent surgery and spent three days in the hospital, with me at her side except for meals and calls. As I write this, we are now twenty-seven years cancer-free and enjoying our grandchildren.

The other call was from retired Vice Admiral Jerry Tuttle, who had been my mentor in the Navy. He was now working for Oracle Corporation as senior vice president for defense business development.

"Eddie, is there any reason why you can't come to work at Oracle?" he asked. I told him that I would need to think about it and discuss with Donna.

"Fine, think about it," he said, "and then be at the Oracle office in Herndon tomorrow morning for an introductory interview. Then we can check off that block and get on with the hiring." Admiral Tuttle didn't do "slow," and he didn't do "later."

The man who had been my Navy mentor would soon become my corporate mentor. I accepted his invitation and informed the Navy. After my retirement ceremony, Donna and I started our transition into a new way of life. After thirty-one years, I would be transitioning from the military world to the corporate world.

★ ★

CHAPTER 11

"HAVE I GOT THAT ABOUT RIGHT?"

Though my colleagues at Oracle Corporation respected my military experience, I soon learned that I would have to earn my stripes in my new role as a business development executive. I needed to show how I could develop business and contribute to business success.

Oracle was an IT market leader with a strong brand. I admired the leadership style of Larry Ellison, the founder. He was intelligently aggressive, highly competitive, and a smart risk-taker. As a leading-edge technology company, Oracle hired the best, the brightest, and the most competitive. To be second place was to be the first loser, and winning was not enough.

I had experience in the small business environment and assumed that success in the corporate arena was just a matter of scale. Many of the success principles are the same, but the complexities of the corporate environment require doing business differently.

The Oracle defense group included retired Army and Air Force Generals and Navy Admirals that made for a small, collegial group. Initially, my accounts included the Joint Chiefs of Staff, Service Health Organization, Defense Information Systems Agency, Contracting Agency, and Military Exchange Services. These accounts were covered by twelve sales representatives and sales consultants. Each of us in Defense was responsible for eight to twelve accounts.

My Internal Strategy

My onboarding was primarily one on one with senior management. They were professional and answered my questions. I made a faulty assumption about my experience and competence to be successful in the corporate arena. There are differences in planning, communicating, and environment.

I identified the key decision-makers in each Oracle DOD account. I learned who could say yes and approve business but equally important who could say no. That just because the boss said "do it" was a far cry from actual execution. Second, I supported presentation key points to describe Oracle solutions. Third, I scheduled office calls to introduce Oracle in terms of customer requirements.

The defense business leaders wanted to know "what do you offer that makes the output of my organization more valuable and how can you reduce my costs." I developed an approach that was slightly different from the classic "you should choose Oracle because we are the best and strongest solution." Inevitably I could see small signs, "tells" that I had shifted the conversation from telling the customer what was needed to explaining our assumptions. I started with their requirements and then how Oracle could best meet those requirements. I would start our conversation something like, "General, here is our understanding of your requirements. Have we got it about right?" Bingo, we start with the customer and not Oracle. Then once we had clarity from the boss, we moved to the next step. "Thanks, we will follow up with some clear solutions for your problems."

My first step was to learn the accounts and the language of information technology and then to meet with the sales representatives to learn their strategies. I first met with their managers to seek their guidance. I figured it would be a good idea to create a presentation to show what I believed would be effective ways to develop defense business. I scheduled a conference room and sent an invitation to all the account managers. Nobody showed up.

I realized my best approach would be to ask questions and listen carefully, looking for guidance on how to best support closing the deals. I scheduled one-on-one meetings with each account manager. They imparted plenty of valuable information, but I didn't hear all that much about the rules for becoming successful or on the specifics of business development.

I was learning an important lesson. When taking on responsibilities, I had to answer two questions: *What does success look like? And how is it measured?* There is power in simplicity. By answering those fundamental questions, you get to the heart of excellence. You know what is expected, and you know when you have achieved it.

My Other Value to Oracle: Mentoring

I was able to mentor account managers and sales representatives, particularly about accepting an offer to work for another company. I would listen carefully and then make an observation or two. I rarely told them what I thought, focusing on open-ended questions and letting them make their own decision. I used the opportunity to help them get more clarity about their decision-making. I always asked if they wanted to leave because of some problem with their manager or Oracle policy. If the answer to either of these was yes, I would advise that whatever was the source of dissatisfaction would be waiting for them.

In Pursuit of Purpose

I believe everyone has a life purpose. I discovered that executive coaching was my real calling in early 2000. I found that no matter how large or small an issue, spending time in solitude and just waiting and listening for an answer for guidance are essential. The guidance does not come for every decision, but when it does come, I listen. Answers often come in whispers and glimpses.

I discovered, however, that those years were a time of preparation on my way to someplace else. I knew in my heart that I would reach the mountaintop one more time in this life, but it would not be at Oracle. I was happy professionally there and found a good measure of success, but what I was doing was just not me. I felt countercultural, as if I were working both sides of the street. Though I believed my work mattered, the question remained: Did I belong there?

Oracle was a stepping stone toward a much better fit for me. For that matter, my Navy career also had amounted to that. Those years, too, were a time of preparation, a prelude to finding my purpose and my passion.

I had to make a choice, and it would be to eventually leave Oracle. I had given a decade to the company already, and I had grown from the experience. It was time now to grow in other ways. Donna and I decided to move to Texas. We long had felt our Texas heritage calling us and to be near Michael, Bobbi, and our granddaughter Casey.

Ashley was initially going to move to Texas with us but decided to stay in Virginia Beach. Soon after our move, we were enjoying our new grandson, Mason.

As we drove "home," I pulled off the highway just after we crossed into Texas from Arkansas. "Why are we stopping?" Donna asked.

"Just give me a few minutes," I said. "I want to get some of this Texas dirt on my boots."

We bought a home near Dallas, and for the next four years, I commuted back to northern Virginia and continued to work for Oracle while continuing my coaching part-time with Oracle's full knowledge. I was not unhappy but bid my final farewell to Oracle in 2008.

My life purpose was confirmed. Now what? My first action was to retain an executive coach. I was private about anything that would be inappropriate and interfere with my responsibilities at Oracle. I hired a business coach to experience coaching. I studied executive coaching online, from books, articles, and conferences. I also enrolled in two business coaching certification courses. I was still guarded but pursued this potential work. After several weeks of online training, I engaged two clients. I did this with full disclosure regarding my qualifications and experience and Oracle. The more I became involved, the more energy I experienced. I would lose track of time, which is unusual for me.

"They're Here! They're Here!"

During those years, we traveled extensively after discovering life on the road in a recreational coach. It took us, and usually our two bichons frises, Beau and Jean Paul, to destinations in Arkansas, Tennessee,

Virginia, Maryland, Florida, Alabama, Mississippi, Oklahoma, Texas, New Mexico, and Arizona.

On one of those memorable trips, granddaughter Casey accompanied us. It was a three-week vacation from Ashville, South Carolina, and Virginia Beach to visit with family and then onward to Pensacola, Florida, with stops along the way.

At Naval Air Station Pensacola on the Gulf Coast, we stayed at an RV park on the beach, at the end of the departure runway of the Blue Angels, the renowned aerobatic squadron. Casey was intrigued at the prospect of seeing them. "That's altogether possible, you never know!" we told her.

As Donna and I were having our morning coffee outside the RV, we heard the thunder of the Hornets as they rolled down the runway and took off. At the same time, the door to the RV flew open, and there was our wide-eyed Casey, who had been sound asleep a moment earlier.

"They're here! They're here!" she shouted, jumping in excitement. And to me, that vision of a gleeful little girl was even more wonderous than the spectacle in the air.

Message to Mason

Let me share with you excerpts from a text message that I wrote to my grandson, Mason. I discovered it in my files as I gathered materials for this book. They reminded me that the qualities of encouragement and gratitude go deep to the heart of what it means to be family.

To Mason:

I'm proud of your continuous improvement in baseball. It is a metaphor for your life. You are entering an important season of life with much opportunity and frequent temptation.

You will continue in this season to make important decisions that will define your future. A wise man once said to me, "Where you will be in five years is heavily influenced by who you hang out with and what you focus on." Seemingly small decisions can form lifetime habits. Go for it in life. Live by values that will make your mom and dad and the rest of us proud of you.

I'm always available to be a resource for you. I know how to just listen. If it ever comes to a point of confusion or uncertainty, call me. Remember that I can't hurt you, but I might help you get clarity.

I love you and am proud of you.—Papaw

My Third Mountaintop: Executive Coaching

Like the first two mountaintops, I felt as though I belonged in the role of an executive coach. This experience was "set apart" from all others.

Executive coaching is about clearly defining personal and professional goals with the metric and/or anecdotal evidence of progress and achievement. Coaching includes assessing strengths, challenges, and potential derailers. All of these are in the context of improving business results, directly or indirectly.

Assessment Phase

I started with the Winslow Assessment, which was developed by business executives and psychology professionals with a focus on business results. It is not a psychological instrument adapted to the business world for hiring and coaching. From the Winslow results, I could define coaching and development themes as well as action plans for stronger performance.

Winslow has also been used to measure sports performance and potential by the MLB for seven years, the NFL for twelve years, and the NHL for fifteen. The Winslow was used to select and develop the 1980 USA Hockey Team who defeated the Russians in one of Hockey's greatest games. It is referred to as "the test" three times in the movie *The Miracle*.

Case Studies

HAWKER BEECHCRAFT CORP.

Donna and I were certified to train coaches to use the Winslow Dynamics assessment and had scheduled a three-day training class in the local area. Donna received a call from a business coach, Stephanie Boisture, requesting information. "Boisture is an unusual name; are you related to Bill Boisture?" "I am," she said. "He's, my husband." Donna knew Bill previously as he was a squadron mate/classmate at the Air Force Academy with Jeff Hurt, Donna's law firm mentor. I knew of Bill's distinguished career as an Air Force fighter pilot who later became CEO of Gulfstream and was now CEO of Hawker Beechcraft Corporation (HBC) in Wichita, Kansas.

Stephanie asked to take the Winslow. She saw the business value and discussed with Bill. He requested that two senior leaders at

Beechcraft take the Winslow to assess the business value. This led to assessing all the HBC leadership team.

Soon I was coaching the Senior Leadership Team (SLT) on an individual basis with emphasis on how they contributed to company's success. I focused on clarity of roles and responsibilities. This is an important coaching topic to explore I find that individuals are not clear about "why am I here" or "what doesn't happen if I don't come to work tomorrow?" After we have clarity on an individual basis, I would do the same exercise, but doing it in pairs, I would have two individuals come to the front of the room. I selected two who work closely together. They would stand in front of the room at the whiteboard; each has a section not visible to the other. Then the discussion began with one asking the other, what so you think my responsibilities are? The answers would be written on the same place but one not visible to the other. The outcomes were always to be interesting. Here were two individuals who work closely together or one reports to the other. You would assume that the lists would be somewhat aligned. Usually there were differences and two very different views. This understanding and greater clarity result in the two working together and achieving greater results. I coached on an individual and team basis for several months with noticeable progress.

One SLT member was just not a fit. He held a senior and essential part of the business. He was talented but had a very sarcastic and condescending attitude. He was very conscientious and professional but could not adjust to new team realities. I gave it a little time and referenced his attitude and that it was not contributing to a healthy business team. The company was operating with slim margins, and there was no room for this type of behavior. I've learned two things about how my clients deal with situations that merit termination. First, they let it go on for longer than I thought was merited, and they made every effort for a positive person to reach the decision on their own. They were very patient and mindful of how difficult this decision could be, and they took it slow in dealing with the individual. But I learned that good leaders let it go longer than merited. In this case, the final decision taken was the right thing to do. Again, it is the mark of positive leadership. The other team members can see this, and that strengthens the culture.

Due to the aircraft market conditions, HBC encountered a challenge that led to bankruptcy. I believed that there would be a successful outcome. Bear in mind this was a business challenge requiring confidence, competence, and experience to make numerous decisions along the way. It was not a single event. My contribution was to observe and listen carefully as decisions were being made. I looked for clear and unambiguous language, communicating with clarity and having the leadership courage to be open and honest with the employees about the current situation. I recall at one point an employee asked in a respectful but nervous way, "Am I going to have a job when this is over?"

Soon HBC faced bankruptcy that lasted several weeks before resolution. I had an unshakeable belief that they would be successful. I observed carefully as the leaders made a wide variety of decisions along the ways. The CEO had the communication style and the courage to be open and honest with the employees about events that were occurring. With expert leadership and management, HBC emerged from bankruptcy and executed a profitable sale.

The SLT took part in an Executive Health program that included a heart-lung scan. While attending a dinner at the Boisture home, Stephanie noticed that I looked gray and lacked my normal energy.

In an email Stephanie sent Donna, she told her what she had observed and that I could take part immediately in the health screening program. Her words were firm but delivered in kindness and concern. Donna made an appointment for the scan for me. After the scan, I returned to the HBC headquarters. The nurse called and said that the doctor would like to see me. "When can you come in?" I said, "How about tomorrow afternoon?" "She said how about right now!" The doctor scheduled surgery for that afternoon but agreed to wait until the following morning so that Donna could fly to Wichita. The scan indicated significant blockage in the lower anterior descending artery, the "widow maker." The surgery was successful.

MANAGING PARTNER SUCCESSION

I also coached a financial services company. The situation was that the managing partner was retiring and wanted to offer his position to one of five partners who were his direct reports. His search included candidates outside the firm, as well. I was hired to coach around the succession process. This was no small challenge because it generated natural strained relations among the five candidates. They were rightfully concerned about an external candidate as well as the competition among the five internal candidates. I did one-on-one coaching with the departing principal as well as each of the five internal candidates. The coaching was a standard engagement with the succession issue a primary but not an exclusive topic. This was one of my "let go of the outcome" strategies. I coached each to prepare their own private assessment of why they were the best choice. Then I had them assess what they had direct control over, such as being the most knowledgeable and best qualified. I coached them to focus on themselves and not the others. That is unrealistic, but it was a reminder that this was a choice of the best suited, which may or may not be them. There was no hard deadline, but the general understanding was about six weeks. The best candidate was selected.

GLOBAL JET CAPITAL

My last coaching client was Global Jet Capital, a company launched in 2016 that specializes in financial leasing and lending solutions exclusively for business jets. My primary focus was to assist in integrating and strengthening a new team of professionals in financial solutions. This new group was composed of two groups from different backgrounds and business cultures.

My first step was to conduct individual meetings and with the input from the Winslow Assessment to define individual strengths and challenges. There was some underlying tension but not in a dysfunctional way. I started with individual reviews and focused on what the two groups had in common. In these individual meetings, I emphasized clarity about differences and developing a common vision and mission.

The potential for strong performance and success was there; it just needed some coaching and focus. In the initial few months, there was only one person who was unable to adapt to a new culture and a new way of doing business. This person was dedicated, professional, and committed to team success but was just not a fit.

This engagement was successful, and most of the heavy lifting was complete by mid-2019. I encountered some health challenges and completed my coaching career at that point.

★ ★

CHAPTER 12

IN SEARCH OF SERENITY

I am proud to have worn the cloth of our nation. From Aviation Cadet to Ensign to Rear Admiral, in the air, on the seas, in the ready rooms, and on the flight decks, I was living my purpose and always thinking "Ready on Arrival to Fight and Win."

An experience in Dallas, back in 2004, gave me a glimpse into what I might experience when passing to the "other side." I went to lunch at a Mexican food restaurant with a couple of my Naval Aviator buddies. I recall the scene vividly as we started sharing stories about the joy and some terror of carrier aviation. Most were true, and all got better with time. Suddenly I felt nauseous and dizzy and felt like I might lose consciousness. It was like nothing I had ever experienced before. I didn't want to be embarrassed in front of my Navy buddies and let them see me that way ("better dead than look bad"). So I excused myself and headed to the men's room. I didn't make it. I went wobbly and sweating profusely and sat against the wall.

I sensed that two or three people were kneeling next to me and were talking, but I couldn't understand what was said. I just sat there and was not anxious but curious. My Navy friends noticed the commotion and came over, laid me on a table, and called 911.

I was in no pain but sensed that something was wrong, perhaps seriously wrong. Was this a stroke or heart attack, and this my last "catapult shot"? An Emergency Medical Services (EMS) crew arrived shortly, put me on a gurney, and rolled me to the big red truck and off to Baylor Hospital we went. One medic stood at my head, and the other by my side. They checked my blood pressure and for symptoms. At the hospital, the EMS head said, "Give him some [*medical Latin word*]." The last words I heard were "sixty over forty"—and then I lost consciousness. I went into what I can only describe as suspended animation and was enveloped by a pure, and I mean pure, white fog. I had no fear or anxiety. I was at peace and felt safe. There was complete silence, and no one or other thing was present.

I was then somewhere else, with a strange sense of consciousness keenly alert with no pain or anxiety. I was thoroughly relaxed and felt safe. The one-word description is *serenity.*

I thought *OK, so this must be what "passing" is like.* For a moment I regretted that I had not said goodbye to Donna but almost immediately felt assured that she would be all right. But I didn't want to go back. I slowly regained consciousness, at peace and back in Texas. Soon the fog lifted, and my reality came slowly but sharply back into focus.

The doctors did several tests and scans and with no explanation. The medical profession can tell us a lot about our bodies, but who can explain such near-death experiences? A dream, perhaps from the medicine whatever drugs they gave me.

My Christian Beliefs

I am committed to a Christ-centered life. Without Jesus Christ, I would be lost in my sinful nature. By grace, I am saved and set free. My decision to follow Him was the most significant and consequential of my life. Nothing matters more.

The central principles of Christian life are as Jesus stated plainly: "Love the Lord your God with all your heart and with all your soul and with all your mind." This is the first and greatest commandment. And the second is like it: "Love your neighbor as yourself."

God expects us to love even those we believe are our enemies. We are to forgive them and pray for them. In the words of Jesus: "I tell you, love your enemies and pray for those who persecute you, that you may be children of your Father in heaven."

That leaves no room for the judgmental hypocrisy that damages Christian witness. "Why do you look at the speck of sawdust in your brother's eye," Jesus said, "and pay no attention to the plank in your own eye?"

There is a difference between knowing about Jesus and knowing Jesus. The latter comes when one experiences the rebirth of salvation. We are saved when we accept that Jesus is the son of God who lived, was crucified, and rose again to bear the burden of our sins and reconnect us with the loving Father.

Heaven is a real place, though it is not defined by time and space. There, God's children will be eternally connected to the Father and Son and with one another. Our bodies will be forever free of disease and pain.

★ ★

RISING FROM HARLINGEN

Much has changed since my boyhood days in Harlingen on the southern tip of Texas. I have special memories of those times of my life. I have some positive regard for my life and experiences there. I don't allow negative thoughts to burden me, but I still remember my experiences there. I look first for the good and ignore the bad. It took a long time, but through much reflection, meditation, and prayer, I learned to surrender and let go of the past.

I have been writing this book for a very long time—for a lifetime, you might say, although it was the summer of 2017 when I finally set to work on it. I found much understanding, resolution, acceptance, letting go, healing, and greater awareness in the significance of revisiting my past. In the six years I spent writing these words, I realized I have been transformed and strengthened, especially in my spiritual life.

The loneliness was a strong motivator for significant success, accomplishment, and leadership. But much of this motivation and dealing with life's challenges came from hubris and defiance of "*Oh Yeah? Watch This!*" I wanted a family, a healthy one where I would belong, be accepted and respected, and I found that in my Navy service. When it was time to move on to the next season, the parting came with pain that lingered for years.

In telling my story of visits to this valley, I learned to look at every day as a new beginning and that I have a choice about today. I set aside the negative and practiced "I'm not perfect but I've learned to express gratitude for the things that are good and praiseworthy." As the years go by and dementia creeps in, I find myself thinking more of what will be.

I wanted to escape the Harlingen of my youth and fly far, far away, and I did. I was looking to the sky from the age of four, when I climbed into a Stearman biplane cockpit with my dad and experienced my first flight. In my first solo flight as a teenager, I got a taste of the serenity that I dreamed would be mine. There would be many more.

In the next dozen years of my youth, I would wash and wax a Stearman, Cessnas, Stinsons, Pipers, Navions, Bonanzas, Aerocoupes. I flew short hops in many of those planes. All of these were a prelude to the F-4s and F-14s that I would fly for three decades as a Naval Flight Officer. I flew at sea and ashore. I commanded a Fighter Squadron, a Carrier Air Wing, an aircraft carrier, and a Carrier Battle Group. As far and as high as I ventured, however, I couldn't leave all my troubles behind.

In my mind's eye, I am departing Harlingen once again—this time not to escape but to explore. I took off on runway 35 at Valley International Airport. The sky is brilliant blue today, and the wind is light as I climb to higher altitudes. I have unlimited visibility. Up here, as on a mountaintop, I have a sense of eternity. I have a view not only of what is but also of what was and what might be.

I pass over the streets and houses of the town I once called home, though it seldom felt that way then. I glance down at the football field and feel as if I am down there now with my teammates, our laughter echoing through the neighborhood. We are sweating it out together, building endurance and character, and fighting off fatigue and pain. We are young and determined, with the will to win.

I continued to climb, and the view of the Rio Grande Valley widens, and I see the farmlands and the highways I traveled many times, some of those hitchhiking when I didn't have the money for a bus ticket to Austin. A scene from long ago returns, and I am down there now with my dad as we travel those roads together. As he drives, I sit quietly, as he utters a few awkward words about Mahalah, my mother, and the pain of the past that bound us. From this height, I have a deeper understanding of a man whose wound never healed, who kept a color photo in his wallet of his beloved young wife and my mother who had long ago had passed.

Onward to Houston, where I see St. Joseph's Hospital, my birthplace. Down there, even now, frozen in time, a newborn baby cries, as does a bewildered young soldier who has no composure as he tries to communicate with relatives and family friends. Eyes of pity look down at this new life, drooling and smiling in a bassinet. *What a shame! Isn't that too bad?*

Could it be that I hear another voice now, rising to the sky? It is faint at first and then clear and resounding. A woman's voice: *This is no shame. This boy is my joy forever, my family, and he will do us proud!* I spent decades striving to prove my worth, only to find that it was never in question. I never got the chance to know Mahalah Hamner Allen. I know now that I will know her always.

Turning northwest, ahead is Hempstead, and I can see the home where Mimi and Papa Joe lived. This is where I spent the first three years of my life until my dad returned from the South Pacific and I was whisked away to live with a few strangers. Now the scenery shifts again, and I am ten, and Mimi is back in my life, and she is showing me a framed photograph of a lovely woman. I am dumbfounded and then devastated.

I fly over the cemetery where my mother, Mahalah, and Mimi lie buried. The only time I saw him cry was when we flew over the Hempstead cemetery. The time will come when I will rendezvous with both of them, and I will thank Mimi for allowing me to be a kid during the joyous summer weeks I spent in this little town. It's as if I'm coming home again, at long last, to the Sunday smell of her pot roast in the oven. And there's the church where she played hymns on the organ—*how sweet the sound that saved a wretch like me!*

One more place to see in Texas—another house, in the town of Trophy Club between Dallas and Fort Worth. Inside, a man of seventy-nine years sits finishing his memoirs, with his gracious wife, Donna, and Schnauzer Jesse Belle at his side. He is writing now about an imaginary flight north from Harlingen. The words come swiftly now. "I turn and steady up on a westerly heading," he writes. "It is time to think about going west."

It's a strange flight plan I follow now. The time, the destination and fuel on board are all coming up "unknown," and yet somehow that doesn't bother me. It's quiet here, and serenity surrounds me. This day is almost too beautiful to comprehend.

I am crossing a desert and farmland. If I proceed to the Pacific Coast, I will be in familiar territory. I will look down and see Naval Air Station (NAS) Miramar and the beaches of La Jolla and Del Mar, and the aircraft carrier piers to the south at NAS North Island. So many memories wait for me there.

Down on the ground, where life happens, I assume positions of great responsibility. I had three successful careers yet learned, in time, that I could not prevail from my own initiative. When we finally let go and confess to God that we feel broken beyond repair, he embraces us with his amazing grace and whispers something like: *"Oh Yeah? Watch This!"*

The good, the bad, the joy, the pain, the highs, and lows—they all come to us in a package. Finally, I have started to unwrap it. I have miles to go on this westerly course and much to see and do before the pure, white fog settles in serenely around me and I will hear the noise no more.

Dad, Lloyd E. Allen, Sr.

Mom, Mahalah Hamner Allen.

Eddie's first flight in a Stearman, c. 1947.

A special time with Mimi, Eddie, and Papa Joe.

High school football, where Ed learned "the game of life."

Eddie commissioning as an Ensign with Col. Gene Allen, USAF, and Mimi.

Mimi and Eddie at his commissioning.

Ed Allen, F-14 Radar Intercept Officer (RIO).

Rear Admiral L. E. Allen, Jr. USN (Ret.)

Captain L. E. Allen, Jr., Change of Command, USS Coral Sea (CV-43).

Personal Files

Ed Allen had 1,223 arrested carrier landings (TRAPS).

Navy photo files, Coral Sea Public Affairs Officer

USS Coral Sea (CV-43) "The Ageless Warrior."

1990 Tailhooker of the Year Award, Captain L. E. Allen, Jr.

Donna and Eddie's wedding, July 8, 1994.

Michael Cook, Donna, Eddie, and Ashley Allen, July 8, 1994.

Special friends and family celebrating Ed's sixtieth birthday.

Donna and Ed on the road in their RV.

Ed enjoying RV life with Beau and Jean Paul.

Donna and Eddie on an Alaskan cruise.

Ed and Donna celebrating Jim's change of command.

Randy and Gerry Fleuriet, Ed and Donna in Paris
for Gerry's surprise birthday party.

Ed, "Bulldog," and Jack Ensch, "Fingers."

Ed's last flight with Bill Boisture in Bill's Cirrus SR22 Turbo.

Ed and Donna at a Red River Rivalry, Texas Longhorns football game.

Ashley Allen Oakley, Luna Mahalah Oakley, and "Papaw" Ed Allen.

Bobbi Cook honoring Ed with a shadowbox of his thirty-one-year career.

Donna's grandchildren Casey and Mason Cook.

Donna's grandson Mason Cook at the National Naval Aviation Museum.

Ed and Donna with Donna's granddaughter Casey.

Casey and Mason Cook celebrating July 4 with "Papaw" Ed Allen.

Mason, Bobbi, Casey, and Michael Cook
at Casey's graduation from Oklahoma State University.

Eddie and Donna at home in Texas.

The President of the United States takes pleasure in presenting

a Gold Star in lieu of the second

MERITORIOUS SERVICE MEDAL to

LLOYD EDWARD ALLEN JR.

CAPTAIN

UNITED STATES NAVY

for service as set forth in the following

CITATION:

"For outstanding meritorious service as Commanding Officer, USS VANCOUVER (LPD 2) from June 1986 to February 1988. Captain ALLEN performed his duties an exemplary and highly professional manner. Displaying exceptional leadership and resourcefulness, he has superbly directed his ship through an arduous overhaul period which included a 112 day shipyard strike and a change of Master Ship Repair Contractors, while maintaining an outstanding safety record. His personal initiative and dedication inspired his crew to perform at a consistently high level, resulting in a superior degree of combat readiness. He personally structured a unique leadership and professional growth program for officers and senior enlisted personnel ensuring the VANCOUVER's preparedness and personnel excellence. Captain ALLEN's professionalism and devotion to duty reflected great credit upon himself and were in keeping with the highest traditions of the United States Naval Service."

For the President,

DAVID E. JEREMIAH
Admiral, U.S. Navy
Commander in Chief U.S. Pacific Fleet

THE UNITED STATES OF AMERICA

THIS IS TO CERTIFY THAT

THE PRESIDENT OF THE UNITED STATES OF AMERICA
HAS AWARDED THE

LEGION OF MERIT

TO

CAPTAIN LLOYD E. ALLEN, JR., UNITED STATES NAVY

FOR

EXCEPTIONALLY MERITORIOUS CONDUCT
IN THE PERFORMANCE OF OUTSTANDING SERVICES
FROM JUNE 1988 THROUGH APRIL 1990

SECRETARY OF THE NAVY

GIVEN THIS   13TH   DAY OF   APRIL   1990

NAVPERS 1650/13 (12-81)

THE SECRETARY OF THE NAVY
WASHINGTON

The President of the United States takes pleasure in presenting the
LEGION OF MERIT to

CAPTAIN LLOYD E. ALLEN, JR.
UNITED STATES NAVY

for service as set forth in the following

CITATION:

For exceptionally meritorious conduct in the performance of
outstanding service while serving as Commanding Officer,
USS CORAL SEA (CV 43) from June 1988 through April 1990. A
superb aircraft carrier commanding officer and inspirational
leader, Captain Allen guided his ship to unparalleled
accomplishments and success during an intensive operating
schedule which included Short Range Attack, Refresher Training,
Restricted Availability, Advanced Phase Independent Ship
Exercise, and a Mediterranean Sea Deployment which saw
USS CORAL SEA perform flawlessly in the Lebanon Hostage Crisis
and in the evacuation of the American Embassy, Beirut. His
tenacity and leadership ensured improvement in all areas of
Ship's readiness and material condition, in addition to
significantly enhancing the crew's morale. Captain Allen deftly
molded the embarked Air Wing and USS CORAL SEA into a smoothly
coordinated, highly effective combat team which proved ready
when called upon to show national resolve. By his superb
leadership, logical judgment, and inspiring devotion to duty,
Captain Allen reflected great credit upon himself and upheld
the highest traditions of the United States Naval Service.

For the President,

Secretary of the Navy

THE UNITED STATES OF AMERICA

THIS IS TO CERTIFY THAT

THE PRESIDENT OF THE UNITED STATES OF AMERICA
HAS AWARDED THE

LEGION OF MERIT
(GOLD STAR IN LIEU OF THE SECOND AWARD)

TO

REAR ADMIRAL LLOYD E. ALLEN, JR., UNITED STATES NAVY

FOR

EXCEPTIONALLY MERITORIOUS CONDUCT
IN THE PERFORMANCE OF OUTSTANDING SERVICES
FROM MAY 1990 TO AUGUST 1991

SECRETARY OF THE NAVY

GIVEN THIS   18th   DAY OF   SEP   1991

THE SECRETARY OF THE NAVY
WASHINGTON

The President of the United States takes pleasure in presenting the
LEGION OF MERIT (Gold Star in lieu of the Second Award) to

REAR ADMIRAL LLOYD E. ALLEN, JR.
UNITED STATES NAVY

for service as set forth in the following

CITATION:

For exceptionally meritorious conduct in the performance of
outstanding service as Commander, Naval Space Command,
Dahlgren, Virginia from May 1990 to August 1991.

Rear Admiral Allen, displaying aggressive leadership and an
extraordinary sense of responsibility in managing scarce
resources, personally made significant contributions which will
have a direct and lasting impact on the Navy's ability to
support space warfighting requirements well into the
Twenty-first Century. He led initiatives to operationalize and
propose baseline training for implementing the space segment of
the Navy's newly designated warfare area of Space and
Electronic Warfare. In addition, Rear Admiral Allen assumed
claimancy for the Space and Electronic Warfare Global
Information Exchange System in the recently developed
COPERNICUS C4I Architecture. His vigorous implementation of
Total Quality Leadership served as a model for other Naval
activities. As Naval Component Commander for Commander in
Chief, U.S. Space Command, Rear Admiral Allen expertly directed
Naval Space Operations during Operation DESERT STORM. At the
outbreak of hostilities, he activated a capable, responsive,
24-hour Naval Space Operations Center which allowed watch
personnel to respond immediately to operational units in
theater. Rear Admiral Allen additionally provided visionary
guidance in leading Naval Space Command in the operation,
training and equipping of space forces to meet the operational
requirements of the Naval warfighter.

Rear Admiral Allen's exemplary leadership, sage judgment,
and inspiring devotion to duty reflected great credit upon
himself and were in keeping with the highest traditions of the
United States Naval Service.

For the President,

Secretary of the Navy

THE UNITED STATES OF AMERICA

TO ALL WHO SHALL SEE THESE PRESENTS, GREETING:

THIS IS TO CERTIFY THAT
THE SECRETARY OF DEFENSE
HAS AWARDED

THE DEFENSE SUPERIOR SERVICE MEDAL

TO

Rear Admiral Lloyd E. Allen, Jr., United States Navy

FOR

EXCEPTIONALLY MERITORIOUS SERVICE
FOR THE ARMED FORCES OF THE UNITED STATES

1 October 1991 to 28 February 1993

GIVEN UNDER MY HAND IN THE CITY OF WASHINGTON
THIS   24th   DAY OF   February   1993

Chairman of the Joint Chiefs of Staff
SECRETARY OF DEFENSE

Citation

TO ACCOMPANY THE AWARD OF THE

𝔇𝔢𝔣𝔢𝔫𝔰𝔢 𝔖𝔲𝔭𝔢𝔯𝔦𝔬𝔯 𝔖𝔢𝔯𝔳𝔦𝔠𝔢 𝔐𝔢𝔡𝔞𝔩

TO

LLOYD E. ALLEN, JR.

Rear Admiral Lloyd E. Allen, Jr., United States Navy, distinguished himself by exceptionally superior service while serving as Deputy Director for Operations (Current Operations), Operations Directorate, the Joint Staff, from 1 October 1991 to 28 February 1993. In this highly sensitive and demanding position, Admiral Allen served as the Joint Staff architect for the development, coordination, and execution of several national policy decisions as well as overall management of critical military operations. During this period, Admiral Allen displayed exceedingly high standards of professionalism, imagination, initiative, and leadership while assisting the Director for Operations and the Chairman of the Joint Chiefs of Staff in the completion of many complex actions leading to the successful execution of Operations PROVIDE COMFORT, PROVIDE HOPE, PROVIDE PROMISE, PROVIDE RELIEF, SOUTHERN WATCH, and RESTORE HOPE. His outstanding professional competence, exceptional grasp of the contingency planning process, and mastery of joint planning had a significant positive impact on national security policymaking. The resounding success of these operations can, to a significant degree, be attributed to the thorough planning, attention to detail, leadership, and unfailing energy displayed by Admiral Allen. The singularly distinctive accomplishments of Rear Admiral Allen reflect great credit upon himself, the United States Navy, and the Joint Staff.